Cyber Selves

Feminist Ethnographies of South Asian Women

Radhika Gajjala

ALTAMIRA
PRESS

A Division of Rowman & Littlefield Publishers, Inc.
Walnut Creek • Lanham • New York • Toronto • Oxford

ALTAMIRA PRESS
A division of Rowman & Littlefield Publishers, Inc.
1630 North Main Street, #367
Walnut Creek, CA 94596
www.altamirapress.com

Rowman & Littlefield Publishers, Inc.
A wholly owned subsidary of The Rowman & Littlefield Publishing Group, Inc.
4501 Forbes Boulevard, Suite 200
Lanham, MD 20706

PO Box 317
Oxford
OX2 9RU, UK

British Library Cataloguing in Publication Information Available

Library of Congress Cataloging-in-Publication Data
Gajjala, Radhika, 1960–
  Cyber selves : feminist ethnographies of South Asian women / Radhika Gajjala.
    p. cm.
  Includes bibliographical references.
  ISBN 0-7591-0691-6 (cloth : alk. paper) — ISBN 0-7591-0692-4 (pbk. : alk. paper)
  1. Cyberfeminism. 2. South Asians—Ethnic identity. 3. Women—Computer network
resources. 4. Electronic discussion groups—Social aspects. I. Title.

  HQ1178.G35 2004
  305.42—dc22

                                                              2004007281

Printed in the United States of America

♾™ The paper used in this publication meets the minimum requirements of American
National Standard for Information Sciences—Permanence of Paper for Printed Library
Materials, ANSI/NISO Z39.48-1992.

Cyber Selves

For my mother.
In memory of my father.

I will always be your impossible dream.

CONTENTS

PART THREE
CYBERFEMINISM AND THE "THIRD-WORLD" DIALOGUES

ACKNOWLEDGMENTS

Like most books, this too is a result of much collaboration, discussion, and exchange of opinions and insights. I have an infinite number of people to thank. If in my haste to complete this document I have forgotten to mention anyone who has contributed to this project, I ask to be forgiven.

The journey started with my dissertation "The SAWnet Refusal: An Interrupted Cyberethnography." I thank the members of my dissertation committee—Roberta Astroff, John Beverley, Danae Clark, and Henry Krips—for being so helpful and for cooperating with me in my efforts at producing the research that began my journeys in cyberspace. They understood what I was trying to do (even at moments when I myself was not too clear on what I was trying to articulate) and supported the unconventional approach and form of that dissertation where (as in this book) in many ways, I audaciously centered myself as an object/subject of (self)-inquiry/interrogation.

I thank all the members of SAWnet, the founders and the moderators (past and present), without whom SAWnet could not exist. But most of all I thank the women (whom I cannot name individually in this document) who started and actively participated in the SAWnet Refusal, as well as the women who critiqued my creative writing posted to SAWnet. A special thanks to the severest critics of both my academic and creative work, for it is my belief that the points of "failure" (the point at which the appearance of coherence and complacency is ruptured) are far more important to the understanding of any project than the moments of actual success. The contradictions are then made visible, allowing us to follow up, speculate, and explore the various hidden and veiled truths and histories that contribute to the situation. Thus, critique, coupled with self-reflexivity, makes possible growth and understanding leading to further conversation and dialogue. This is not to suggest that the encouragement and praise was not equally necessary or helpful, of course.

In addition to all the above, I would like to thank several people who commented (during conference presentations, on online forums, via e-mail, and in graduate seminars) on my academic and creative work at various stages in the process of my attempts to articulate the ideas in this book. They all encouraged me to continue working on issues addressed in this book project, convincing me of their worth in various ways by giving me different suggestions, perspectives, mentoring, validation, encouragement, and insights. I will list the names of at least some of these people: Deepika Bahri, Kalpana Biswas, Susan Chacko, S. Charusheela, Nicole Constable, Dwight Conquergood, Laurie Cubbison, Shamita Das Dasgupta, Jerry Everard, Carole Farber, Sarah Hodges, Laura Kipnis, Enok Knippersund, Barbara Lazarus, Lee-Ellen Marvin, Robin Means-Coleman, Vagdevi Meunier, Shalini Puri, Manjusree Sen, Sangeeta Ray, Alan Sondheim, Valerie Staats, Carol Stabile, Charles Stivale, Fiona Steinkampf, Judith Tabron, Saadia Toor, Margaret Trawick, Jyotsna Vaid, Kamala Visweswaran, Robyn Warhol, Steve Jones, Sara Ahmed, Karen Riggs, Mia Consalvo, Susaana Paasanon, Faith Wilding, Kay Picart, Ellen Berry, Bryan Taylor, Kirsten Broadfoot, John Warren, Julie Burke, Annette Markham, Barbara Monfils, Deborah Gordon, and the anonymous reviewers of the proposal for this book as well as several members of SAWnet whose names I am not at liberty to reveal. I also wish to thank members of various electronic lists for providing me with insights into the nature of the virtual community, the discursive subject and interpersonal interaction online. The various lists are sa-cyborgs, Third-World women, postcolonial, women-writing-culture, seminar-13, Cybermind, FOP-L (Fiction-of-Philosophy List), and Gender and Postmodern Communication. In the list world, I especially want to thank the members of the Spoon Collective (especially Malgosia Arkansas, who has been instrumental in encouraging and helping me, with her amazing technical know-how, in setting up my various Spoon Collective lists and projects).

Since moving to BGSU, I have received various kinds of support from colleagues, students, and friends. I want to thank them all; I have learned much from conversations with them. The members of the Institute of Culture and Society writing group (especially Vicki Patraka, the Director of the Institute) and the members of transnational research cluster and cultures of technology researcher cluster—I thank them for feedback and suggestions through this process. Department chairs, colleagues, and mentors—Lynda Dixon, John Makay, Don Mcquarie, Al Gonzalez, and Melissa Spirek. My hardworking RAs over the last six years—YuShi, Omedi Ochieng, and Qi Tang; special colleagues, friends, and collaborators Kris Blair, Bettina Heinz, Denise Menchaca, Jillana Enteen, Melissa Altman, Melanie Fields, Leesha Thrower, Shawna Woody, Christine Pease-Hernandez, Yahui Zhang, Chris Bollinger, and especially Annapurna Mamidipudi, my coauthor over the past seven years. To my AltaMira editors, Rosalie Robertson and Grace Ebron, as well as others who helped edit the manuscript, I am extremely grateful for gently guiding me through the process of book publishing. The spaces I inhabit—both online and offline—are strewn with stray lines of writing, pieces of paper with writing on them, notebooks with self-reflection and commentary—very much like my father, I have made a habit of writing myself into the margins, cracks, and crevices of the mainstream—tired at the thought and immensity of the translation tasks entailed in writing the self for all those audiences. . . . I would never have been able to sustain the effort of putting some of my work together in the form of a book without the understanding cooperation of these editors, my family, colleagues, mentors, students, and friends.

A special thanks to Uma, Padma, Sarada, Sridhar, Suvarna, Kiran, and Sathyakrishna for inspiring much of my creative work just by coming into the world and being precious to me, and in the case of several of them, being patient with my online and face-to-face monologues regarding my research. Their lived contexts and experiences as highly educated Indian women and men within Indian social contexts have enriched both my academic work and my creative work by deepening my understanding of some of the complex issues involved in representing non-Western contexts within a Western field of knowledge and power.

Finally, I wish to thank more of my family.

My mother (Smt. V. Satyavati) and my eldest sister (Dr. Subbalaxmi) contribute most strongly to my feminism. My mother's experiences and struggles, as a comparatively less-educated woman and as a traditional Indian woman who struggled and amazingly negotiated various sociocultural situations in her life as she traveled different parts of the world with my father, contribute very strongly to my understanding of how oppressive a Western feminist and modern woman ideology (as they functioned in the sixties and seventies and as they function even today) can be to many Third-World women. My eldest sister's struggles, on the other hand, as a modern professional woman confronting traditional sociocultural expectations while juggling her personal and professional life contribute to my feminism in another way. From these two strong, unique, and sensitive women, I learned lessons of strength, courage, and perseverance.

To the male role models in my life, my father (V. N. Murti), my eldest brother (Krishna Vedula), and brother-in-law (A. Venkatesh), I owe a special debt. My nationalism, idealism, and absolute down-to-earth practicality are partly what I gained from them.

The rest of my siblings (Murali, Ratnamala, and Kasturi) contributed in an infinite number of ways by both encouraging and challenging my thought at every stage. I thank all my sisters, brothers, brothers-in-law, sisters-in-law, nieces, and nephews.

Most importantly—I couldn't have started or finished this project without the constant support and understanding of the two most important people in my life today, my husband (Venkat/Vinnie) and my son (Pratap).

Credits

Chapters 1, 2, and 3 are drawn from my dissertation: Gajjala, R. The SAWnet Refusal: An Interrupted Cyberethnography. Doctoral diss., University of Pittsburgh, 1998. *Dissertation Abstracts International* (UMI No. 9900131) (1998). (Chair: Roberta Astroff.)

Chapter 3 was first published as: Gajjala, R. An Interrupted Postcolonial/Feminist Cyberethnography: Complicity and Resistance in the "Cyberfield." *Feminist Media Studies* 2, no. 2 (2002). Reprinted by permission of Taylor and Francis Group, PLC, http://www.tandf.co.uk.

Chapter 4 was first published as: Gajjala, R. Interrogating Identities: Composing Other Cyber-spaces. *International and Intercultural Communication Annual* 25 (2002). Reprinted by permission of Sage Publications, Inc.

Chapter 6 was first published as: Gajjala, Radhika, and Annapurna Mamidipudi. Cyberfeminism, Technology, and International "Development." *Gender and Development* 7, no. 2 (1999). Reprinted by permission of Taylor and Francis Group, PLC, http://www.tandf.co.uk/journals/carfax/13552074.html.

PROLOGUE
I REFUSE TO BE READ

From: gajjala+@pitt.edu Fri May 30 08:23:25 1997
Date: Fri, 30 May 1997 07:30:59-0400 (EDT)
From: bhaatasari
Reply-To: sa-cyborgs@jefferson.village.Virginia.EDU
To: sa-cyborgs@jefferson.village.Virginia.EDU

Over space and time
this moment
            i *refuse* to
be read.
the lines of my palm
tell me things
perhaps
            the lines of my jaatakam
                        tell me things perhaps
but by you
i *refuse* to be
read
                        these alien words
cannot convey
            your desire will
interpret
most definitely

awry

[that's not what i *meant*

damn you!]

i refuse refuse

to be

read

by you!

Yet i know i must write

for you

if i am to write

at

all

to exist at all

my words always thinking of you

and what you will think of me

but for the moment

i *refuse* refuse

REFUSE

to be read

by you

the way you would

like

to read me

just because it's easier for

you

within your way of thinking and

feeling

to read me

like that.

oh how i hate you

for doing this to my

word

yet i shall come

back

again and again

hoping to be understood

Understood as even i sometimes

don't

hoping to spark just a little
bit . . .

hoping that the signifiers i use
will
slip
and
trip

      your mind

so that what i am trying to signify
gets across to you
            someday?
not always falling within
the
colonial
desire
always
within
the male
desire

         exoticizing myself
         out of habit

habit—formed the day i was born
into what i was born. . . .
where i was born . . .
         but today
i take pleasure
in refusing
you.
            —Radhika, May 30, 1997

INTRODUCTION

B roadly, this book examines online community formations in relation to the subjectivities produced at the intersection of technologies and globalization. It is written in three parts to show the
progression of my engagement with issues related to South Asian cyber-
spaces, feminist cyber(auto)ethnographies, designing and building cyberfeminist webs, and Third-World critiques of cyberfeminism. Part I is a
mapping of the transition from "Cyborg-Diaspora to the SAWnet Refusal"; thus, the book begins with a discussion of South Asian community
formations online, specifically in relation to technology and gendered subjectivities in the context of globalization, studying online spaces and engaging issues related to the designing of online communities and feminist
safe spaces online. While examining subjectivities that emerge in cyberspace at the intersection of the local and global, "virtual" and "real," I also
engage methodological and theoretical issues raised for Internet studies of
such online communities. One of the unique features of studying online
communities is that we can simultaneously and actively produce online
communities while studying them. This means that the cyberethnogra-
pher (i.e., an ethnographer studying cyberspaces) can build the techno-
social spaces and invite people to inhabit such spaces while engaging in
collaborative studies of such spaces. Thus the two chapters in Part II are
based in cyberethnographies that result from my attempts at building
South Asian cyberfeminist webs. The latter part of the book—Part III—
engages discussions of issues raised at the intersection of westernized
knowledge production systems, communities of production and practice

1

outside the logics of multinational corporation and consumption in relation to the information communication technologies (ICTs) and their design. Thus, the two chapters in Part III are coauthored with Annapurna Mamidipudi.

Following my dissertation experience with a South Asian Women's e-mail list (SAWnet), I have focused some of my research efforts on examining the production and design aspects of building online communities (see http://www.cyberdiva.org). In the process, I have been researching other e-mail lists (founded and maintained by me) such as the Third-World women list, women-writing-culture list, and the sa-cyborgs list (see http://lists.village.virginia.edu/~spoons for information on these lists). Thus this work expands existing debates regarding cyberspacial and academic representational practices by examining specific sites of "silence" and "speech" performed online. Therefore, in this body of work, my collaborators and I ask: Who speaks online, why, when, and how? Who is absent? Who counts as a netizen? What communities of practice and production shape and are in turn shaped by the Internet and associated technological environments? Is "cyber culture" an empowering culture in any sense?

Overall, the chapters in this book explore various theoretical and applied concerns that arise in attempts to design and produce South Asian cyberfeminist e-spaces. Such attempts must inevitably negotiate diasporic and nationalist gender, class, religious, and caste identity formations as well as online corporate and academic cultures situated in an increasingly global economy. In addition, they must also negotiate liberal cyberfeminist celebrations of technology as empowering to all women.

This work on "cyber selves" is thus unique and different from several feminist analyses of women-centered e-spaces that exist (Herring 1996; Warnick 1999; Spender 1995) because it engages with the specific context of my intervention as a researcher and includes a discussion of the response and interactions of list members to being researched. Further, the book extends the debates at the intersection of cyber culture, feminism, and globalization by discussion of real-world contexts of access and hegemony that shape virtuality. Thus in the last two chapters of this book (coauthored with Annapurna Mamidipudi) there is a juxtaposition of "old" and "new" technologies in an attempt to highlight and problematize various celebratory discourses about "ICTs" as empowering to all. The situations discussed in the chapters of the book demand the interrogation of the processes and assumptions behind academic feminist ethnographies and examine the implications of such debates for the study of Internet spaces. The chapters also highlight issues related to the politics of enunciation within diasporic spaces. Issues of voice and voicelessness as well as of marginalization, ventriloquizing, and Othering based on gender, race, class, and geographical location emerge as central concerns.

The chapters in this book can be read as interrelated—following major themes in relation to feminist cyberethnographies, South Asian digital diasporas, and "Third-World" critiques of cyberfeminism—but they can also be read and used as discrete essays for particular class syllabi as necessary. This project spans a period of eight years of research (pre- and postdissertation) conducted by me in relation to the Internet, women, and globalization and is an intervention in the field of postcolonial feminism as well as in the field of New Technologies.

In chapters 1 and 2, I chart out my point of entry into the study of online spaces and describe how my project transitioned from Cyborg-Diaspora, which was a project exploring the imagining of virtual community and the (im)possibility of dialogic encounters online, to "The SAWnet Refusal." Chapter 3 discusses feminist research and methodologies that inform the study of online spaces as well as the problems faced by feminist researchers concerned with notions of location of the researcher. This chapter reviews and extends available literature in relation to ethnographies of Internet spaces and feminist approaches to the study of electronic spaces through continued reference to issues raised by the SAWnet refusal. This chapter also situates my research on feminist e-spaces in the context of feminist media studies. It is true that there is now (in the year 2004) an increasing, even overwhelming, amount of research being done regarding the Internet (feminist, critical, and mainstream). However, in the early 1990s Internet researchers had very little to draw on in terms of prior studies to inform the methodologies used to study sociocultural formations online. My work on SAWnet, for instance, began in 1994 amidst much hype (even among critical researchers) regarding virtual community and hypertext (see Landow 1992 and Rheingold 1991). At the time, there were few precedents available on what it might mean to "study" a dynamic Internet community from a postcolonial feminist perspective.[1]

The experience of SAWnet refusal raises a number of important questions central to the main thesis of the book and some of these are explored and extended through other cyberethnographic case studies in the rest of the chapters. How do ethnographic practices and the ethnographer evolve in an online context? How are they revolutionized? What constitutes the field and how do we define the boundaries of the field? Further, can we transpose concerns that arise out of RL ("real life") anthropology or face-to-face ethnography onto the study of virtual communities without seriously considering the very important differences in the nature of face-to-face interaction and virtual interaction and thus confuse the issues? When can "RL" anthropological and critical issues be considered relevant to online ethnography? (see Jacobson 1999 for a discussion of some of these issues). Considering the interactive nature of online participation, questions arise as to who is an ethnographer, who qualifies to be a "native" informant, and what the options are for refusing to be a subject. I explore some of the possible reasons for my failure to do a cyberethnography in this particular situation. I also focus on the ways in which conducting ethnography in cyberspace is distinctly different from "real-life" ethnography while also underscoring some issues/problematics that are specific to the technology/medium.

Chapter 4 situates the Internet in relation to intercultural communication, South Asia, and South Asian diasporas, emphasizing the importance of discourses online as discursive representations. In this chapter I attempt to lay out frames and theoretical lenses that are provided by postcolonial, feminist, and diaspora studies scholars in writing about South Asians in digital diaspora and how they might help shape the practical activity of trying to build subaltern technological counterspaces. Thus, I begin to carve a theoretical path leading to connections between available approaches to the examination of South Asians in cyberspace. The attempt is based in efforts to further the lines of inquiry and discussion that would lead to the design and building of projects that theoretically and practically connect specific community needs and technologically mediated environments (such as the Internet) in order to make technological design work for marginalized populations of the world.

Chapters 4 and 5 engage my own efforts to design list spaces in an effort to build cyberfeminist webs. Thus, in chapter 5, I examine case studies based in interactions on the sa-cyborgs list, and in chapter 6, I examine case studies based in the Third-World women list and the women-writing culture list. I founded all three of these lists in an effort to examine the emergence of gendered subjectivities in Internet (technologically) mediated spaces.

Chapters 6 and 7 introduce my coauthor Annapurna Mamidipudi in an effort to juxtapose different contexts of technology use to highlight the problems of the development models that see ICTs as transparent and empowering across class, caste, geography, gender, race, and so on. Chapter 6 is a reprint of an article Annapurna and I published in 1999, and chapter 7 is a performative piece pointing to the problems we face in trying to articulate our concerns within a globalized academic space. The book ends with an epilogue—a poem written by me as I was preparing to defend my dissertation.

The Veiling of the Subaltern and the "Right" to Speak

The present work is not about "the subaltern." It is about the privilege of being able to speak, to write. Yet it is also about the silences—the unsaid and the cannot-be-said. Not only is it about what "position[s] of authority we have been given,"[2] have taken, or have been enabled, and at whose expense we speak, but implicitly it is also a questioning into how we might be able to negotiate from within our speech and our silences in order to transform or disrupt hegemony. It is about negotiating from within the hegemonic and about attempting to disrupt hegemonic narratives. It is about resistance and complicity. Once again, I emphasize that this work is *not about "the subaltern."* But it is about not remaining silent in the face of the imagined "subaltern" at the same time as it is about trying not to silence voices of dissent. As a member of SAWnet pointed out in response to one of my papers, "[i]f we remain silent, that is not going to make the subaltern heard." However, it is important for us to examine the speaking roles we are assigned as well as the location from which we speak. While the nonsubaltern South Asian woman, as the "Other" of the Western woman, finds a point of entry into the hegemonic sphere, in itself enabled by a history of relative cultural and material, she must remember that her speech could be used as representative of a subaltern who is not located within the same sphere of material and cultural privilege. As Deepika Bahri points out, then, this

> "other" (who has not spoken so far, only been spoken about) [who] begins to gaze at herself in the hope of reopening examination, ... must acknowledge the power of this gaze, the context of its production, the privilege implied in the right to speak at all, as well as the limitations of that can be known or said. (Bahri 1994: 9)

A work that examines bourgeois discourses like the ones reproduced online within so-called postcolonial virtual spaces could potentially lead to the line of questioning that would interrogate and problematize roles assigned and assumed (voluntarily and involuntarily) by immigrant Third-World subjects. Working-class diasporic women and a majority of the women within the *real* geographic Third-World locations pay the price for the discourses produced by bourgeois diasporic postcolonials, who are viewed by the Western world as ideal informants because of their/our ability to translate ourselves and our Other so that we fit appropriately within hegemonic structures of power and thought. Discourses thus produced perform a "veiling" function in relation to the materially and culturally underprivileged subaltern populations.

I must assert, however, that the solution is not for the relatively privileged Third-World subject to silence herself in an effort to avoid speaking for the subaltern. While suggesting an interrogation of the roles assumed by and assigned to the Third-World woman and/or feminist, within the Western hegemonic sphere, my intention is not to dismiss her speech as untrue and invalid. I suggest that we should clarify the *difference* in the speaking locations of Third-World subjects (whether feminist or not) situated within a setting of material and cultural privilege that is not available to subaltern women situated elsewhere geographically, materially, culturally. My intention is not to deny the struggles of diasporic Third-World women. As "C," a member of SAWnet points out,

> The question about "what is *our* right to speak?" while it *looks* like a question that places the Subaltern/Other on the map, doesn't after all produce the spaces *from* which the Subaltern could speak. . . . Instead of ending with "From what position of authority would *we* speak?" I'd

phrase question more explicitly as "who is paying the *price* for this authority and *whom* am I taken to be speaking *for*? *What* did we *say* when we were given/took up the authority to speak? And *how* did we say it?"

Macherey points out that "[s]ilences shape all speech" (Macherey 1986: 85), and it is the silences of the subaltern that shape bourgeois speech. But can speech "reveal . . . silence" (Macherey 1986: 86)? And if silence is indeed revealed does this mean that the speech itself is invalid? According to Macherey, the attempt to reveal the latent (the silent):

> simply means that the latent is not another meaning which ultimately and miraculously *dispels* the first (manifest) meaning. Thus we can see that meaning is in the *relation* between the implicit and explicit, not on one or the other side of the fence. . . . What is important in the work is what it does not say. This is not the same as the careless notation "what it refuses to say" . . . what the work *cannot say* is important, because there the elaboration of the utterance is acted out, in a sort of journey to silence. (Macherey 1986: 86–87)

In the face of my subjects' refusal, I have to leave some things unsaid. The conditions of the production of this work as it is also do not permit "everything" to be revealed. There is much that is lost in the translation.

This work, then, is a struggle. To borrow Stuart Hall's phrase, it is my way of "wrestling with angels." Hall writes that "[t]he only theory worth having is that which you have to fight off, not that which you speak with profound fluency" (Hall 1992: 280). I use theoretical frameworks in my struggle to articulate a position within the academy, within society. Whatever position gets articulated—whatever the reader reads into what I write—my struggle with theory continues.

Part of this struggle for me in trying to articulate a position within the academia is with academic form within hegemonic structures of knowledge. The struggle with form is also the result of having to write about a medium of the future (electronic Internet texts) while the legitimacy and value of academic production is still embedded in the longstanding academic tradition of the print medium. Therefore, the form and method of this work is unconventional.

Notes

1. I use the term both in relation to temporal consciousness and epistemological concerns arising from the notion. See Bahri and Vasudeva 1996 for further discussions of the notion of "post-colonial/postcolonial."

2. This phrase is taken from a response by a SAWnet member. I refer to the SAWnet member as "C."

Part One

CYBORG-DIASPORA TO THE SAWNET REFUSAL

IMAGINING VIRTUAL COMMUNITY AND DIALOGIC ENCOUNTERS

Cyberspacial Beginnings

I suppose you could say I have been a traveler in cyberspace since 1993 when I actually began using my university e-mail account for more than just the exchange of personal e-mail, by subscribing to e-mail discussion lists and perusing Usenet newsgroups. In February 1994, I became a member of the e-mail discussion list for South Asian women called SAWnet (the South Asian women's network) and a little later, I volunteered to be one of the moderators for SAWnet. In summer 1995, I set up a website of my own and in fall of the same year, I became a member of the Spoon Collective[1] after taking over the duties of comoderator for the postcolonial list and founding the Third-World women list. Later, I started a discussion list concerning South Asian Women's identity on seminar-13, a temporary discussion space offered by the Spoon Collective. Seminar-13 is now known as sa-cyborgs. Later, in 1996, I started the women-writing-culture list. My e-mail and World Wide Web ventures have opened many doors of opportunity for me both personally and professionally. However, my initial fascination with cyberspatial existence is now strongly tempered with a certain amount of cynicism and even anger at the hegemonizing/colonizing tendencies of mainstream scientific and technological discourses that dominate and structure the use of Internet communication. I have since coauthored several critiques of liberatory discourses regarding cyberspace (see chapters 7 and 8 for more on this).

In 1993, when I first came across newsgroups like SCI (soc.culture.indian) and e-mail discussion lists like SAWnet I was also studying issues related to the imagining of nation in graduate school. I became curious about how the imagination and thought of postcolonial men and women in diaspora formed online networks while inhabiting certain spaces on the Internet. I began spending long periods of time online, examining some online communities formed around notions of ethnic/regional/linguistic/religious/national identities. These social formations in cyberspace are embedded in real-life diasporic communities and identity formations. I began with the question of who (if anyone) was being empowered by the existence of these online communities, and if anyone was being empowered in any sense, how were they being empowered. At that time, my examination was focused on two online groups—the Usenet newsgroup called soc.culture.indian (SCI) and the women-only e-mail discussion list called the South Asian Women's network (SAWnet).

Soc.culture.indian

Soc.culture.indian is a "Group for discussion about India & things Indian."[2] It is a newsgroup that can be accessed, read, and contributed to on the UNIX system. It is also accessible via the World Wide Web. The messages from Usenet newsgroups such as SCI are available through the Dejanews search engine.[3]

SAWnet

The women-only South Asian Women's network (SAWnet) was formed because women's issues are often marginalized and sometimes even belittled on Usenet groups like soc.culture.indian. On July 31, 1995, according to the statistics posted by one of the moderators[4] of the group, there were 320 members. More than 250 of these members appeared to be in the United States and about 25 were in Canada (guessing from the e-mail addresses). The majority of the women on SAWnet appear to be professionals and academics living in the United States and in Canada. In 1997 there were over 600 members subscribed to SAWnet.

According to the website, "SAWnet (South Asian Women's network) is a forum for south asian women, and those interested in issues relevant to south asian women" (see http://www.umiacs.umd.edu/users/sawweb/

sawnet/ for a complete description) and the "mailing list is restricted to women only by the consensus vote of the members."

Cyborg-Diaspora: Virtual Imagined Community

In my early work on SAWnet, I used the term "cyborg-diaspora" to refer to the formation of virtual imagined communities of diasporic postcolonials online. Cyborg-diaspora is a term used by Indira Karamcheti (1992) in her review of the book *Reworlding: The Literature of the Indian Diaspora* edited by Emanuel Nelson. She writes of a possible community through technology,[5] which will help disrupt the fossilization of "Indianness" within Indian diasporic communities. This fetishized notion of "an 'Indian' essence that survives all vicissitudes of changing material and cultural circumstances" (Karamcheti 1992: 269) creates a shared diasporic sensibility and is the result of a community created through memory.

The disruption implied by the term cyborg-diaspora can occur if there are counternarratives of present real-life material, social and cultural conditions within the geographical region mapped out as "India." The counternarratives to those offered by most diasporic Indians, who live in communities created through memory, could come, for example, from Indians actually living in India, as well as through cross-generational and across rural-urban and class/caste narratives. For instance, in his study of a discussion group of people from the Indian state of Orissa called OR-NET,[6] Anustup Nayak suggests that cross-generational interactions on diasporic South Asian networks can be constitutive of "cyborg-diaspora" (see Nayak 2002).

Imagining Virtual Community

Ananda Mitra, while describing interactions on SCI, suggests that national formations of postcolonials online are:

> product[s] of people who make up the electronic community, and given the wide range of opinions and worldviews proposed on the Internet, the image of India that is produced on SCI for its users is replete with contradictions that are a mainstay of everyday life in the South Asian country. (1997: 71)

13

However, it is my contention that the existence of these contradictions alone does not ensure a disruption of hegemony. Hegemony operates through the appropriation, "incorporation and neutralization of contradictions, not on a purely monological discourse" (Beverley 1993: 25). The few counternarratives produced by men and women located geographically, intellectually, professionally, ideologically, and socially outside of the bourgeois/elite westernized postcolonial worldview (a worldview that is often uncritically complicitious with Enlightenment and colonial worldview in relation to "progress" and the Third World) risk being subsumed, appropriated, outnumbered, and even silenced.

Thus cyborg-diaspora, instead of being disruptive in the sense suggested by Karamcheti, continues to reproduce a shared diasporic sensibility based on nostalgia for an imagined "India" but this nostalgia shifts generationally. However, it is true that, in many ways while diasporic communities continue to be, to a large extent, communities created through memory, online diasporic communities tend to be caught in shifts and encounters between nostalgia and "the real" in conversation as men and women from various geographical locations log onto these e-spaces. I would still argue, however, that cyborg-diaspora as it exists now does not successfully disrupt narratives constructed through nostalgia and the "mummification of tradition" (Bhattacharjee 1992) that continue to shape transnational South Asian diasporas. As Archana Sharma argues (see Sharma 2003), South Asians in fact are complicitous in the production of whitened cyberspace. In her work, Sharma examines the "racing" of cyberspace in relation to South Asian social collectivities as a "race" imagining community, and argues that:

> South Asians occupy a particular kind of native identity and their racialization is complicated through and upheld by class positioning. I would like to suggest that such a positioning points to a desire for whiteness. (2003)

Further, as Maria Fernandez suggests, the electronic revolution has "imperialist underpinnings" (1999: 38). Thus, cyborg-diaspora does not necessarily imply that the virtual communities created by postcolonials, whether the members are situated geographically in the West or in the Third World, are communities of resistance to hegemonic structures of westernization and modernity.

In his work on virtual community, Howard Rheingold, who is generally very upbeat about the possibilities of Internet and virtual communities, cautions us that "virtual communities could help citizens revitalize democracy, or they could be luring us into an attractively packaged substitute for democratic discourse" (1991: 276) points out, the logic of late capitalism functions through a continual generation of novelty (Jameson 1991).

In talking of cyborg-diaspora, I use the term "imagining" in two ways. One is the imagining of community online. As one of the SAWnet members who responded to my request for feedback commented, we imagine our readers/audience when posting within an online community, we imagine the members of the community. We imagine a kind of affective "communion." This imagining does not have to relate to our real-life communities or other imagined ones.

The other sense in which I use the term imagine in relation to community is an adaptation of Anderson's (1991) definition of "imagined communities." Thus nationalism is maintained through a sharing of beliefs and symbolic constructs as much as through geographical alliances and communal identities, and media play a key role in the circulation and sharing of such alliances, creating an "imagined" community of people around the world.

This type of imagining applies in the case of creation of virtual communities framed around national, linguistic, ethnic, religious identity/subject formations. As Mitra writes:

> The "imagination" that binds the members of the electronic group is the common memory of the same putative place of origin from which most of the posters c[o]me. The sense of community is based on an original home where everyone belonged, as well as a sense of a new space where the question of belonging is always problematized. Since the original home is now inaccessible, the Internet space is co-opted to find the same companionship that was available in that original place of residence. (1997: 70)

In this sense, SAWnet is an imagined virtual community of South Asian women based on the imagined possibility that they share many common issues, experiences, and beliefs.

When home is no longer a concrete geographical place and exists within the "two-dimensionality of memory and nostalgia" (Karamcheti 1992), as is the case for the diasporic postcolonial, cyberspace may provide a way for disembodied minds (at both intellectual and affective levels) to make contact with apparently similar "beings." With the increased availability of Internet tools, "a future when diasporic identity is created by technology—a cyborg-diaspora" (Karamcheti 1992) could become more than a science fiction narrative for immigrant and exile communities. Although I would hesitate to claim that diasporic identity could ever be *created* by technology, I do agree that the expression of identity is enabled in various ways by access to technology and the medium, which in turn shapes the perception of diasporic identity. Further, diasporic identity has always been mediated and shaped in interaction with various available technologies. In a sense, the existence of diasporic imagination and community is indeed heavily reliant on various forms of media and technologies for travel, archival, storage, and communication. The collective imaginations of the people involved will be restricted by what is perceived as their material, social, cultural, ethnic, religious, geographical location. The Internet communities I refer to in this work are imagined virtual communities, "almost" communities based on the imagined possibility that they share common experience, "media-scapes" and "idea-scapes" (Appadurai 1990).

Dialogic Encounters?

Linda Alcoff has suggested that "existing communication technologies have the potential to produce" what she refers to as "dialogic encounters" (1992: 23). A dialogic encounter, according to Alcoff, occurs when we replace the practice of speaking for the other with the practice of speaking to or with others. Alcoff derives this notion from Spivak's article "Can the Subaltern Speak?" where the latter critiques Foucault and Deleuze's position in their discussion on "Intellectuals and Power." Speaking to and with instead of *for* the other "still allows for the possibility that the oppressed will produce a 'countersentence' that can then suggest a new historical narrative" (Alcoff 1992: 23).

Although I doubt that access to communication technologies at present is widespread enough for this to happen on a large enough scale across various economic classes and geographical regions, I would like to believe that every now and then, dialogic encounters at least begin to happen through Internet communication. Particularly, interactive online spaces and interfaces such as e-mail lists, blogs, and multiuser synchronous spaces enabled by MOOs, MUDs, MSN messenger, AOL chat, IRC, and even some computer games online might, under certain conditions, have a potential for providing a space for dialogic interaction. I must point out, however, that although there is a proliferation of contradictory discourses on the networks I refer to in this work, it is the bringing out into the open and close examination of the so-called contradictions that might possibly lead to dialogic encounters. The mere coexistence of contradictory and various discourses does not guarantee a dialogic exchange. My investigations in relation to this led me to start various online dialogue-spaces using a variety of interfaces, and I have discussed these efforts later in this book.

Notes

1. Spoon Collective is a group of netizens hosting several discussion lists. It is operated through the Institute for Advanced Technology in the Humanities at the University of Virginia. Our website is at http://jefferson.village.virginia.edu/~spoons. When I began this list (then called "Representing") from my e-mail account at the University of Pittsburgh, Alan Sondheim, the owner of the Cybermind list and Fiction-of-Philosophy list, suggested that I propose my list to the Spoon Collective. I thank Malgosia Arkansas of the Spoon Collective and Alan Sondheim for their help and support in my efforts to start and maintain my lists.

2. http://www.lib.ox.ac.uk/internet/news/soc.culture.indian.html.

3. http://www.dejanews.com/.

4. She gave me written permission to quote from any of her posts to SAWnet in early 1994, when I first began to study the discussion list.

5. And by technology, she does not mean computer technology and Internet technologies alone. She refers to communication technologies "ranging from the ease of telephone communication with India, to the availability of cultural productions like movies, television and radio programs, art and performance, to safer, faster, and cheaper air flights" (Karamcheti 1992: 262).

6. See http://www1.cs.columbia.edu/~deba/ornet/ornmain.shtml.

THE SAWNET REFUSAL

In an effort to examine the possibility of dialogic encounters on a South Asian Women's Network, I began an open-ended "study" of the e-mail discussion group in summer 1994. My purpose was to see how the proliferation of often contradictory discourses produced a text concerning the South Asian woman's identity in diaspora, as well as her struggles regarding feminist discourses. I wanted to see if it was/is possible for the privileged (only women with material privilege had access to the Internet) South Asian woman to produce her own countersentences to narratives regarding her identity—thus finding a "space" to speak from. I also wanted to understand if indeed she had found such a "space"—what the implications of her speaking within such a space were. For instance, what complicities and resistances get articulated through the struggles for control over meaning making in such spaces? Who is absented, disappeared, and silenced, and why? What are the implications of gaining voice through certain classed, gendered, and sexualized routes? Because this is a "community" (though in several ways different from a "real-life" (RL) community, the "virtual community" is imbedded in real-life communities), I expected that there were/are several discourses being marginalized. Thus my project was also to study what kind of discourses/opinions were being marginalized or silenced in this Internet community.

Prior to my decision to write about SAWnet, I was already a very "vocal" member (since late January 1994). I was known to the participants of this group as a fiction writer and a poet who often wrote in what some labeled as a stream of consciousness style. My constant interruptions—posting of my poetry and "prose"—were welcomed by some and were irksome to others. Most of my work deals with identity probing in diaspora and some may be seen to have a feminist "flavor" (depending on who's reading), and there were several members of the group who indicated that some of my work "spoke" to their experience.

My attempts at studying this group took several forms. In summer 1994, I started by posting a survey on SAWnet with the intention of finding out how the nature of the online community had changed since the time of its formation. At this time I mentioned my intention (based in my past as a freelance writer for magazines and newspapers in India) of writing at least a magazine article about SAWnet. The interest in the changing nature of the group led me to try to find out if any members felt dissatisfied with how the group was interacting. I wanted to see what kinds of discourses were being marginalized. This led me to try to investigate the possibilities of dialogic interaction within an online community like SAWnet.

All this while, I was aware of the rule on SAWnet that posts could only be shared with nonmembers of SAWnet if the poster gave permission. I had asked and received permission to use the posts I had used in my paper. I did not imagine that writing a description of SAWnet would be a problem for any of its members, since this does not involve the use of anyone's messages on SAWnet.

In spring 1995 an anthropologist from New Zealand (a non-South Asian)[1] announced her intention of writing a paper about the community. She contacted some members of SAWnet personally, to ask for permission to use our posts.[2] She announced her decision to study SAWnet and to write a paper about SAWnet (as I had done earlier on in 1994). This started a series of discussions about the value of studying a group like SAWnet. Some women protested. They wanted to be "left alone" in what they perceived as a private space. Discussions began to get very interesting and even heated. I decided to remind members of SAWnet that I too had been writing about SAWnet as part of my dissertation project since 1994. My entry into the discussions regarding SAWnet contributed to and further complicated the discussion. One or two members of SAWnet asked to see our work. I had already planned to invite reactions to my paper in the long run, but the discussions on SAWnet just speeded things up a little. The anthropologist from New Zealand and I sent out papers to at least fifteen members of the group. Mine was an almost completed paper that I was revising with the aim of eventually trying to publish.

During the discussion, a message was posted by an anonymous poster who informed the participants of SAWnet that she had been studying the various writing styles of the members for a while. She claimed that she had done a "psychiatric" analysis of various contributors based on their writing styles and wished to publish an article based on the study. She later confessed that this was a prank. However, I think this brief intervention made many participants even more aware of how little control they/we might have over how our posts would be interpreted and used by researchers and over the general findings of studies conducted about SAWnet.

The discussions led to a vote. This vote decided not to allow anyone to make "global statements" about SAWnet—that is, "no one is allowed to generalize based on any of the posts on the discussion list."[3] We would need to obtain permission from individual members if we wished to use their messages. The current SAWnet policy statement linked to the SAWnet website records this policy decision (see http://www.umiacs.umd.edu/users/sawweb/sawnet/).

The three options suggested and voted for were:

1. Studies of SAWnet are specifically forbidden.

2. Studies of SAWnet are permitted, as long as no post is quoted without explicit permission from its author.

3. SAWnet should be studied, but SAWnet members together will choose someone to study us. Only that person has the authority to do the study.

There were about 350 members at the time of the vote. Sixty-nine of the members voted. Thirty-nine out of this number voted for option one, twenty-nine voted for option two, and one person voted for option three.

The paper I e-mailed to some SAWnet members contained an analysis of South Asian women. The description of South Asian women was mainly derived from the works of scholars like Partha Chatterjee, Chandra Mohanty, Uma Narayan, Kum Kum Sangari, Sudesh Vaid, Uma Chakravarti, Lata Mani, and Gayathri Spivak, who deal mainly with Indian women.[4]

I positioned Indian women as being faced by the "dark side of epistemic privilege" (Narayan 1990: 265). I wrote that Indian women are faced with the tension between Indian nationalism's discursive positioning of the "Bharatiya Nari" (Woman of Bharat/India) and Western feminism's complicity with colonial discourses. The Indian woman's expression of agency is complicated by the fact that both these discourses speak *for* and *about* her, but do not allow her to speak for herself. My study was partly an attempt to see what kind of subject positions were allowing the South Asian woman to speak for herself as an acting agent.

In this same paper, I discussed the proliferation of discourses (which were often contradictory) on SAWnet regarding the educated/professional South Asian woman's position within Western and South Asian societies. I argued that the discourses on SAWnet indicate that it is not possible to use one single general description of the identity of SAWnet members or of South Asian women.

In an attempt to describe some of the contradictory discourses, I used a particular example. This example referred indirectly to discussions regarding the place of feminism within the lived contexts of some of the outspoken members on SAWnet and the manner in which they represented their views regarding lived contexts of South Asian women in general, which in turn were based on their personal perceptions regarding the South Asian community in diaspora. While showing that the virtual community of South Asian women certainly marginalizes certain types of discourses, the example that I used was also an attempt to highlight the fact that the westernized, economically privileged South Asian/Indian women were not to be considered representative of South Asian women in general.

I argued that, while this so-called community of South Asian women does indeed have a potential to provide a space for "dialogic encounters" (Alcoff 1992), it could also end up as a mere gathering of some elite South Asian/Indian women, marginalizing those who might pose a challenge or threat to the Indian immigrant society's vision of itself as the ideal immigrant community in the United States. However, to be fair to the participants on SAWnet, I must point out that the range of opinions is very broad and that members do often critique each other's views.

In my discussion of the particular example (although I had permission from the woman whose example I used as part of the discussion, I have decided not to describe that example in detail in the present work), I used Chandra Mohanty's article "Under Western Eyes: Feminist Scholarship and Colonial Discourses" (1994) and Linda Alcoff's article on "The Problem of Speaking for Others" (1992).

Chandra Mohanty analyzes the production of the monolithic notion of Third-World women in certain feminist texts published by Zed Press. She names analytic categories that are employed by these feminists. Her effort in trying to point out the appropriation and codification of stories of Third-World women by First-World feminist interests is part of her project of trying to form strategic coalitions across class, race, and national boundaries. She traces a series of effects that result from the assumptions made by feminists using "the west" as the primary referent in their theory and praxis. She argues that the analytic principles used by such "Western feminists" (a category that includes non-Western women as well) end up distorting feminist political practices and limiting any possibility of forming strategic coalitions. She argues that there is an "urgent need to examine the political implications of our analytic strategies and principles" (Mohanty 1994: 196). Although she focuses on work by white feminists, she clearly states that the analytic strategies that she pinpoints in her essay are also used by westernized postcolonials in their work on issues dealing with women of lesser privilege.

Alcoff discusses the epistemically significant impact that the location of a speaker has and the issues that it raises. She argues that it is not possible to avoid any form of epistemic violence simply by refusing to speak for the Other. She argues that there is a need for spaces where dialogic encounters might be made possible. Rather than speaking *for* others, she believes it would be better to speak *with* others. She suggests that classrooms, hospitals, workplaces, welfare agencies, universities, and the like may provide these spaces. She also hints that communication technologies may have the potential for making possible these dialogic encounters.

My description of South Asian women and the discussion and representation of it on SAWnet caused some controversy, and some of the reactions of South Asian women both on- and offline point out the need for a non-Western feminist critique of Chatterjee's work in particular. My own complicity, as creative writer and an academic, in producing certain images of South Asian women also becomes an issue to be interrogated.

Thus my focus was now on a community that was suddenly faced with the fact that a women-only e-mail list is not necessarily a safe space or a private space, despite the rule on SAWnet that "posts are private and should not be forwarded without the author's permission." The implicit protection promised by such a rule seemed to have lulled the participants into thinking that the e-mail discussions were like conversations in a friend's living room, where their privacy could not be invaded by unwanted researchers or nasty encounters that might have real-life consequences beyond the artificial boundaries of cyberspace. My project therefore shifted from the examination of cyborg-diaspora in relation to SAWnet to what I began to refer to as "the SAWnet refusal."

Betrayal?

Judith Stacey has pointed out how "[p]ersonal interests and skills meld, often mysteriously, with collective feminist concerns to determine a particular topic of research, which, in turn, appears to guide the research methods employed in its service" (Stacey 1988: 22). The present work brings together my interest in South Asian identity formations, feminism, critical ethnography, creative expression, and the communication medium that is known as the Internet. The interrogation of the SAWnet refusal is partly an excuse for me to try and examine various issues that concern me as a (diasporic) South Asian woman of privilege, writing from within a field of power that is within the West (John 1996). On the Internet, the interactions by diasporic intellectuals and professionals are clearly within the field of power controlled by Western hegemonic structures of thought and education. These online performances serve as "represent[ation]s [of] the world to the West" (Everard 2000: 57). As Jerry Everard points out, "the Internet is far from global, but it serves to appropriate the idea of the global for western consumption. And there is a human cost to this process" (2000).

Therefore, I proceeded to interrogate the SAWnet refusal and some creative and academic texts produced within the context of a virtual community (see Gajjala 1998 for more on this). The situation I interrogated arose out of my interrupted cyberethnography of SAWnet. The study of SAWnet was to be a part of a larger project that would focus on the centrality of notions of gender and sexuality and the importance of representations of the "subaltern" in the formulation of these online group identities. The work now concerns a community (SAWnet) that has not authorized me to represent them/us. I have produced what Belsey refers to as an "interrogative text" (1986: 85).

When I first joined SAWnet in February 1994, I did not join with the intention of studying the group. I heard about SAWnet by word of mouth, from some Indian friends. Prior to joining SAWnet, my use of the Internet was fairly limited. But once I became a member, I began to actively participate in discussions. I even started to share my fiction and poetry, and I felt very much a part of this "community." SAWnet is a community of real women who use the Internet to communicate opinions, thoughts, and feelings to each other. Within this community, I found an audience for some of my thoughts and feelings with regard to being a South Asian living outside of her home nation. The community viewed in this manner is not "virtual" but very real. Much of the debate surrounding the question of whether community is possible in cyberspace implicitly assumes that real and virtual—RL and cyberspace—can be separated during online interaction (see Gajjala 1998 for a discussion of these issues).

The approach I took to the attempted study of the South Asian women's group and my present work draws from work by postcolonial feminists. This very approach arises out of the dilemma faced by diasporic and black women in relation to community/national identity. But what does it mean to speak from a non-Western feminist perspective? The very notion of an educated postcolonial woman of privilege taking up a non-Western perspective has been problematized in works of people like Chandra Mohanty and Gayatri Spivak. Non-Western feminists, writes Narayan:

> must think and function within the context of a powerful tradition that, although it systematically oppresses women, also contains within itself a discourse that confers a high value on women's place in the general scheme of things. . . . The imperative we experience as feminists to be critical of how our culture and traditions oppress women conflicts with our desire as members of once colonized cultures to affirm the value of the same culture and traditions. (1990: 259)

Before I go any further with this discussion, I need to problematize my use of the phrase "South Asian." The main reason for my use of the term, of course, is because the online group that I discuss in this work is labeled a South Asian community. The description of South Asian women that I use in the present work is in actuality based on academic work mainly to do with Indian women both inside and outside of the United States. Annanya Bhattacharjee explains her use of the term South Asian in her recent essay "The Public/Private Mirage: Mapping Homes and Undomesticating Violence Work in the South Asian Immigrant Community" (1997). While discussing the use of "'South Asian' as identity and as community," she writes that the:

> label's attraction for South Asians such as myself lies, to a large extent, in its ability to subsume more than one nation. It is thus seen by those skeptical of oppressive conditions of nationhood as something less rigid; it has little institutional authority (such as a flag or an embassy) and less solidified cultural homogeneity. In the competing ethnic realities of the United States, it is also a way to amass numbers. (1997: 309)

My use of the label South Asian is in a similar vein. However, I am more concerned about the use of the label by online diasporic formations like SAWnet. While the intention in naming SAWnet as the South Asian Women's Network may have been to forge strategic coalitions between women of that region, it may be that among the active participants,[5] there is a hegemony of diasporic *Indian* women.[6] This could be seen as a replication of Indian hegemony in relation to other South Asian countries, since India is often seen by its neighbors as imperialist. There is a hegemony of Indian intellectuals and of studies concerning India even in the area of South Asia Studies, and the fact that the scholarship available to me is mostly by and about Indian women could "convey overtones of domination and exclusion" (Bhattacharjee 1997: 309). This is not intentional on my part. In fact when I began a study of SAWnet, one of my main goals was to see who and what viewpoints were being marginalized during SAWnet discussions.

My attempts at interrogating texts that I produced on SAWnet are not to try and reveal a "true" South Asian identity or to establish my authority as a representative South Asian woman. I am attempting an examination of the process of production of some of the texts that were placed before members of SAWnet. This entails, among other things, an examination of the form in which the work was produced, the audience for whom it was produced, as well as the ideology implicit in the narratives produced.

Notes

1. JV, a member of SAWnet, writes, "I wonder if the vehemence of the reaction to your wanting to study SAWnet was not in part exacerbated by the fact that just around that time (or was it before your query) the white (?) researcher had wanted to do so as well."

2. She asked permission to quote some of my creative work, and of course I gave her permission.

3. Since there was no statement that suggested that the rule does not apply to the moderators who set up the SAWnet website, perhaps it could be argued that the description of SAWnet at the website does not comply with this rule. Or is a website not a published document? Or perhaps the rule does not apply to descriptions written before the vote was taken? In this case, my description of SAWnet should not be subject to the vote either.

4. I do not wish to suggest that only Indian women are South Asian women, or that it is possible to describe all South Asian women's experience based on the study of Indian women. I am definitely problematizing the current hegemony of "India studies" under the head of "South Asia Studies."

5. By "active participants" I mean the members of SAWnet who are not "lurkers" (that is, silent members, who rarely or never post messages on SAWnet, but who subscribe to the e-mail discussion list).

6. At least this is what I suspect based on my observation of SAWnet between the period of March 1994 and September 1995.

CHAPTER THREE
FEMINIST ETHNOGRAPHY, FEMINIST MEDIA STUDIES, AND INTERNET RESEARCH

The "SAWnet refusal" raises complex issues in relation to feminist ethnography and feminist Internet research. As described in the previous chapter, in spring 1994, I began to research a South Asian women's e-mail discussion list. In summer 1995, this study was interrupted (this is what I refer to as the "refusal") and my attempt at studying the group failed. However, the discussions leading to the failure highlighted several important issues in relation to ethnographic practices online and in relation to feminist practices of representation that I explore here.

How do ethnographic practices and the ethnographer evolve in an on-line context? How are they revolutionized? What constitutes the field and how do we define the boundaries of the field? Further, can we transpose concerns that arise out of RL (real-life) anthropology or face-to-face ethnography onto the study of virtual communities without seriously considering the very important differences in the nature of face-to-face interaction and virtual interaction and thus confuse the issues? When can RL anthropological and critical issues be considered relevant to online ethnography? (See Jacobson 1999 for a discussion of some of these issues.) Considering the interactive nature of online participation, questions arise as to who is an ethnographer, who qualifies to be a "native" informant, and what the options are for refusing to be a subject. For instance, in my experience with the SAWnet list, I was an active participant posting fiction and poetry, having a common ethos with other list members, and thus, in many ways, considered "an insider." It was only when I announced my researcher role and the SAWnettors began to consider the implications of being written about that I became somewhat of an "outsider." The medium (the Internet with its lack of face-to-face contact), the transnational nature of access to the community I was studying, and the fact that I had been a participant on SAWnet since 1993 and a South Asian woman further complicated the ethnographic experience. There was yet another complication to online ethnography related to the matter of feminist e-spaces—what does it mean to define a "safe" women-only social space, what are the inclusions and exclusions implicit in the notion of being "safe" online, and who speaks for who and so on? Because of these and other contradictions that emerged in this situation, my efforts at studying the group failed.

Specifically, the experience highlighted for me some of the ways in which conducting ethnography in cyberspace is distinctly different from real-life ethnography while also underscoring some issues/problematics that are specific to the technology/medium.

Feminist Media Studies and Cyberethnography

Concerns raised by my experience with SAWnet are not new to feminist media researchers who have undertaken ethnographies of popular culture audiences. Some concerns that arise in my work also are ones faced by scholars such as Andrea Press and Liz Cole (1999) during their encounters with audiences. Researching women's ideas regarding abortion debates and their sense of identity as formed through interpersonal dialogue and exposure to cultural images on television and other mass media, they faced certain challenges. For instance the need to examine their "own unvoiced experiences" and worldview in relation to that of their subjects (Press and Cole 1999: x). The challenges that they faced have their basis in the contradictions between the feminist ideals of empowerment, protection, empathy, and understanding of women on the one hand and the "objectivity" demands on researchers on the other. These challenges led to an interrogation of their positionality as researchers and as feminists. They were faced with having to make choices for which their academic, scholarly "methods" literature and training had not prepared them. "On their [i.e., the subjects'] territory, in their homes," write Press and Cole, "we were stripped of authority and the illusion of objectivity." In addition, their "subjects had in effect restored our subjectivity, thereby complicating the whole practice and meaning of research" (1999: ix). Their experiences highlighted the fact that researchers' subjectivities are produced within historical and structural constraints, making it impossible for them to adopt a "view from nowhere" stance. The importance of contextual, self-reflexive ethnographies examining the political economy and cultural dynamics of the Internet (cyberspace) cannot be overstated.

In the case of the SAWnet refusal, a project that began as an attempt to study South Asian women's use of and inhabitation of the Internet resulted in a situation in which a variety of issues were raised that problematized and rearticulated concerns central to feminist ethnography and the politics of the Internet. Both Internet researchers and feminist researchers face issues related to subjects "talking back," questioning and displacing the researcher's authority. In the case of feminist researchers, this occurs because of the contradictory demands between feminist ideals of dialogic engagement and the implicit need for the researcher to hide her subjectivity in an effort to seem "unbiased." In the case of research conducted in Internet spaces, the interactive nature of the medium potentially leads to a questioning of the researcher's conceptual and methodological assumptions by "subjects."

Concerns and dialogues regarding women-only safe spaces originating in second-wave feminisms are played out in various ways in relation to women and cyberspace. There is a body of work examining women's use of the Internet that invokes past feminist debates regarding the need for safe spaces for women, while engaging and questioning the (im)possibilities of safe women-only spaces online. For instance, researchers such as Kristine Blair and Pamela Takayoshi (1999) and several contributors to their volume on "Feminist Cyberscapes: Mapping Gendered Academic Spaces" argue that "websites written by and for women that offer women spaces for active participation in the construction of more productive, supportive, and encouraging subject positions for women and girls" (Blair and Takayoshi 1999: 6).

Feminist researchers of the Internet have also examined such processes of inclusion and exclusion where the creation of a supposedly safe space for specific groups of women leads to exclusionary, homogenizing identification practices that are oppressive to certain members of the groups (see Addison and Hillgoss 1999; Gajjala 2001).

Feminist Internet Research Methodologies?

It is true that there is now an increasing, even overwhelming, amount of research being done regarding the Internet (feminist, critical, and mainstream). However, in the early 1990s Internet researchers had very little to draw on in terms of prior studies to inform the methodologies used to study sociocultural formations online. My work on SAWnet began in 1994 amidst much hype (even among critical researchers) regarding virtual community and hypertext (see Landow 1992 and Rheingold 1991). At the time, there were few precedents available on what it might mean to "study" a dynamic Internet community from a postcolonial feminist perspective.[1] My initial attempts therefore drew on a combination of survey methods and textual analyses.

Although "method" for Internet studies and for doing research in cyberspace (Jacobson 1999) is still much debated and discussed (see, for example, discussions on lists such as A(o)IR), there are several prior studies for feminist researchers of the Internet to draw on now: Usenet groups; Web-based "communities"; MUDs and MOOs (see Gurak 1997; Boese 1998–2000); textual and discourse analyses of websites (Blair and Takayoshi 1999); adolescent girls (such as the "Cybergrrls" phenomena) and their access to the Internet and technology (Sauer 2001); rhetorical analyses of women-centered sites (Warnick 1999); and so on. Further, feminist researchers have examined Internet presences of women from a variety of disciplinary and cross-disciplinary perspectives, nonetheless broadly working on issues to do with the Internet and women. These are feminist researchers, for instance, whose work is categorized as being about computer-mediated communication and women (Herring 1996); cyberfeminisms (Wilding and Fernandez 1999; Hall 1996; Gajjala and Mamidipudi 1999; Sunden 2001); women in development, globalization and women (Harcourt 1999); feminist Internet studies (Van Zoonen 2001); race, gender, sexuality, and cyberculture (Heinz, Li, Inuzuka, and Zender 2002); digital labor and women (Biemann 1999); and so on. Of course all these labels and categories are probably individual negotiations of disciplinarity as many feminist scholars are required to situate their work and justify it within authorized "disciplines."[2] It is not my intention to provide an extensive detailing and critique of the literature available but to point to some of the diversity of feminist perspectives on studying the Internet currently available.

Feminist/Postcolonial Media/Communication Research

My work is situated at the intersection of feminist media studies and post-colonial communication research. While I draw much of my theoretical insights from postcolonial theory and subaltern studies (Spivak 1994; Spivak and Grosz 1990; Narayan 1990; Chatterjee 1989; Bhattacharjee 1992, 1997; Mohanty 1993, 1994; Sangari and Vaid 1989), feminist cultural anthropology (Behar and Gordon 1996; Visweswaran 1994; Stacey 1988; John 1996), and feminist philosophy (Alcoff 1992; Code 1998; Narayan 1990; Harding 1998), concerns related to "speaking for," "speaking to," "speaking with," and "speaking about" human subjects of research are not unknown to feminist Internet researchers (see Augustin 1999). For instance, Laura Augustin raises the following questions regarding Internet access:

> Some of those excluded from much of mainstream society want to include themselves in this new technology, whatever it turns out to be. They see themselves as protagonists of the revolution. But what of those who are excluded and who see nothing (so far) about this new technology to attract them or who do not know it exists? Should they be forced to be included, if being included could "help" them (acquire useful information, tell their stories and educate others)? (1999: 152)

In an attempt to examine my relations with the women I was writing about, I asked questions about my own location within the South Asian diasporic community. How did my own "discrepant dis-locations" (John 1996) and personal history within Indian society and Indian diasporic communities affect my approach to an ethnography of South Asians? What were my hidden presumptions/assumptions and biases? "Contrary to the assumptions that brought some of us to the United States," writes Mary John in relation to her own experience as an anthropologist of South Asian origin researching members of a South Asian community in the United States:

> we may thus find ourselves forced to contend with our places of departure, asked to function as native informants from "elsewhere." From what position of authority would we speak? The very attempt to become such cultural representatives, the faltering of our memory, must, then,

lead to a different realization: the need for an examination of the historical, institutional, and social relations that have, in fact, produced subjects also quite unlike "the native informant" of old. (1996: 23)

Questions regarding ethnography and representation are complicated
by the nature of the medium for communication, which blurs various categories such as public/private, audience/author, producer/consumer, and
text/human subject. For example, there was some confusion on the part of
SAWnet members with regard to SAWnet interactions being texts. If I
had been studying documents written by these women and published in
printed form, there would have been no doubt about the documents being texts. However, while studying texts produced in interaction on e-mail
lists, the researcher necessarily takes on an "approach in which the object
of study is a process (the changing text) rather than a project (the static
text)" (Aarseth 1994: 82).

My work regarding SAWnet has always tried to respect members'
wishes by not using messages about personal lives without their permission. My intention, contrary to what some SAWnet members may have
suspected, was not (and still is not) to write an exposé of the South
Asian female mind and life. It was also never my intention to expose any
confidences members may have shared about their private lives. Judith
Stacey, in her article "Can There Be a Feminist Ethnography," suggests
that the feminist ethnographer's dilemma is that "feminist researchers
are apt to suffer the delusion of alliance more than the delusion of sep-
arateness" (1988: 22). The ethnographer, in such cases, "betrays" (and
perhaps even feels betrayed by) a feminist principle and by the subjects
of her ethnographic study. In such instances, there is no getting away
from the fact that:

> feminist goals of "authenticity, reciprocity, and intersubjectivity" might
> be even more dangerous than the masculinist, objectifying methods they
> criticize, precisely because professed beliefs of mutual respect are apt to
> hide relations of authority, exploitation, and manipulation unavoidable
> in fieldwork. (John 1996: 118)

However, feminist ethnographers such as Behar and Gordon (1996) and
Stacey (1988) have also argued for the necessity of a dialogue between

feminist ideals and ethnographic methodologies, engaging postmodern approaches that emphasize the partialness, situatedness of any type of representation, while underscoring the power relations at play in the very process of representation (see Behar and Gordon 1996).

Feminist Betrayals?

In the case of my attempted cyberethnography of SAWnet, I tried for heteroglossia by inviting responses to my work on SAWnet. I e-mailed a paper to some SAWnet members that contained an analysis of South Asian women when discussions that led to the refusal began in 1995. In that paper, I had positioned Indian women as being faced by the "dark side of epistemic privilege" (Narayan 1990). I wrote that Indian women are faced with the tension between Indian nationalism's discursive positioning of the "Bharatiya Nari" (Woman of Bharat/India) and Western feminism's complicity with colonial discourses. The Indian woman's expression of agency is complicated by the fact that both these discourses speak *for* and *about* her, but do not allow her to speak for herself. My study was thus an attempt to examine the emergence of the kinds of South Asian female subject positions that were enabled within the context of SAWnet and how agency was discursively negotiated by individual posters.

My description of South Asian women and of SAWnet caused some controversy. In this instance then, my own complicity, as creative writer and an academic, in producing certain images of South Asian women also becomes an issue to be interrogated. I interrogate my own complicity by examining some texts produced by me in relation to SAWnet in previous work (Gajjala 1998).

The objections to my study of SAWnet revolved around questions regarding methodology, concern over privacy, and concerns about how I would represent the members of SAWnet. The questions regarding methodology were mainly focused on a science versus nonscience debate. The members who questioned my methodology wanted to know how I would "validate" my findings and make sure that I was presenting the "correct" picture of SAWnet, since my audience might not be able to verify the truth of what I was saying by accessing the archives of SAWnet.[3] JV, a

35

member of SAWnet who responded to several drafts of my work before and after the SAWnet refusal, writes:

> Looking back, I feel that the debate that ended in the decision for "the vote" arose largely because some of the dominant personalities at the time were resistant to others' attempts to characterize the South Asian women's community (or at least the community comprised of sawnet-tors) . . . perhaps out of a somewhat naive fear of mis-representation, or out of a distrust of (and disdain for?) the field (and jargon) you represented. That is, in addition to other variables, the debate was very much also one of the "proper" way to do "scientific" research (I remember at least the most vocal opponent was in the hard sciences).

Some women did not think I should be representing them and making generalizations about their lives. They felt that what I had written was not their experience. Most importantly, they were concerned that my narrative regarding South Asian women would be received as representative, whether I intended it to be so or not. There was a strain of anxiety over the possibility that my disclaimers would make no difference to an audience that would readily generalize based on one or two academic studies.

Some of the women who were objecting to the study appeared to have felt betrayed by a comember (not just as a comember of SAWnet, but a comember of the South Asian community). During discussions that occurred after some members had read the papers that I and another researcher (who was a non-South Asian academic woman) had e-mailed to them, several issues concerning power and representation were raised. These reactions highlight several important questions concerning broader, contemporary issues raised in critical, postcolonial ethnography and feminist anthropology. Especially since, as JV suggests, "the vehemence of the reaction [could have been] in part exacerbated by the fact that just around that time the white (?) researcher had wanted to do so as well"—which once again invokes controversies and discussions ongoing within feminist theory and anthropology about the politics of location and representation of Third-World women and black women by white feminist ethnographers.

Kamala Visweswaran (1994) has suggested that ethnographers need to consider ways to "disrupt" their own authority as ethnographers, thus allowing for a questioning of the work. In her essay "Betrayal: An Analysis in Three Acts," she argues for a deconstructive ethnography, where the ethnographer pays careful attention to silences, refusals, and betrayals. How is a "disruption of authority" possible? As a participant ethnographer and as a Third-World academic producing my work within the Western academy, my encounter with SAWnet raises several concerns about audiences. Visweswaran discusses (in the context of her work as a feminist anthropologist) the struggles and difficulties she faces as an intellectual who locates herself "in a field of power (the West) and in the production of a particular knowledge (about the East)" (Visweswaran 1994: 25). She advances the case for "a critical feminist epistemology that finds its stakes, as with other interested and subversive epistemologies . . . and, as Haraway puts it, 'situated knowledge'" (1994: xx). Kirin Narayan, another anthropologist concerned with issues related to participant observation, argues for the "enactment of hybridity in our texts" (1997: 23; emphasis in the original). This hybridity is intended as a negotiation between "the world of engaged scholarship and the world of the everyday" (Narayan 1997). Narayan writes:

> What we must focus on is the quality of relations with the people we seek to represent in our texts: are they viewed as mere fodder for professionally self-serving statements about a generalized Other, or are they accepted as subjects with voices, views, and dilemmas—people to whom we are bonded through ties of reciprocity and who may even be critical of our professional enterprise? (1997: 23)

These and other related strategies are useful for the ethnographer who is a participant-observer. But how would I build this "quality of relations" with women I know mainly (if not solely) through my e-mail communication with them? Consequently, one of the steps I took was to continually share my drafts of this work with women who were willing to respond publicly to my call for participation. I also tried to supplement e-mail interaction with face-to-face encounters with South Asian women. I have shown drafts of this project to several South Asian women both in the United States and when I visited India. I have incorporated critiques I received as part of an interrogation of my academic and creative work about South Asian women into the study (Gajjala 1998).

It was my face-to-face meetings with several SAWnet members at The South Asia Conference 1996 that made me rethink my position with regard to SAWnet. I met SAWnet members there who were very interested in the project. I don't think they were all necessarily in favor of it, but in my face-to-face meetings with these women, I could see them more as multidimensional human beings than reading their posts on SAWnet had allowed for. I saw these women who might not want to be fitted into a complete "yes" or absolute "no" answer.

What then does "betrayal" mean in the context of SAWnet as a virtual community? For Stacey "fieldwork represents an intrusion and intervention into a system of relationships, that the researcher is far freer than the researched to leave. The inequality and the potential treacherousness of this relationship is inescapable" (1988: 23). In the case of a virtual community, however, both the researcher and researched are free to leave. As Ananda Mitra points out, "there is no Internet audience[/participant] who is also not empowered to become an agent to mold the space as he or she wishes" (1997: 60). In the case of the real-life community that this virtual community (SAWnet) is imbedded in, neither I as researcher nor my resistant subjects can "leave." Undoubtedly, my work is an intrusion and an intervention into a system of relationships as they existed prior to discussions about my study in fall 1995. It might even be considered an invasion of privacy of sorts. However, it is not an intrusion and intervention in the sense that it would be if I were doing an ethnography of a RL community. In fact from what I can see, the posters on SAWnet continue with no obvious "institutional" memory of having been "intruded upon" as new members generate discussions on topics similar and dissimilar to what has been discussed on SAWnet since nearly a decade ago, and old members continue to participate.

This confusion between "real" and virtual spaces continues even in current debates concerning privacy on the Internet. Internet exchanges are very often assumed to be like telephone exchanges or personal (hardcopy) letters. We tend to forget that, unlike our telephone interactions, our online interactions are recorded in print, they are stored in a system that can be accessed by system managers and hackers. They can be retrieved and viewed any time in the future.

What is also important to note here is that hardly any of the women on SAWnet are likely to be materially or culturally "underprivileged." Unlike in the case of anthropology of the materially and culturally "Other," virtual presence—the very fact that someone is online and actively participating—situates the ethnographic subject in a social space of material and cultural privilege with access to the same power structures as the researcher. They, as much as I, are anthropologists reporting not just about our own diasporic communities within and outside of our communities as participant-observers, but also "anthropologists in reverse" (John 1996: 18) who carry back "field notes" about our host society/culture to our birth-countries. As I have argued elsewhere, e-mail lists, Usenet bulletin boards, websites, web-conferences, and so on can be regarded as ethnographies of the self and of the other.

> SAWnet itself [i]s a space of representation. This is by virtue of its being a discursive space that depends on some shared conceptions of identity—imagined, as you note. . . . In effect, SAWnet itself exists because of our self-representations within real life communities AS S. Asian women. ("C" as quoted in Gajjala 2002: 190)

Our narratives are often appropriated and reappropriated in various ways within the hegemonic frameworks that favor "Western" structures of thought and cultures. Our words are quite often given more weight than those of a less culturally/materially privileged woman speaking from the geographical Third-World. The attribution of "authenticity" to our narratives and the investment of various audiences (First-World "global" policy makers, for instance) in naming our narratives as those of the "unheard" must be questioned.

Sara Suleri, Trinh Minh-ha, and others have discussed the process by which non-Western (nonwhite, nonbourgeoisie) women are "Othered" and "interpellated by difference" (John 1996). At the same moment as we are "Othered" we also learn to be the ideal Other, complicitous with the existing status quo and the process of "Othering" men and women of lesser material and cultural privilege. As the representative native informants or ideal reporters from the Third World who have been indoctrinated into the cultural and linguistic system through our postcolonial education and our "sanctioned ignorances" (John 1996), we learn to produce narratives about our so-called Othered selves that will fit appropriately within hegemonic narratives concerning Third-World cultures. It is this habitual, even unwitting, complicity that needs to be interrogated.

Further, as a member of SAWnet pointed out in response to one of my papers concerning SAWnet, "[i]f we remain silent, that is not going to make the subaltern heard" ("C" as quoted in Gajjala 2002: 190). It is therefore important for us to examine the speaking roles we are assigned as well as the location from which we speak. While the nonsubaltern Third-World woman, as the "Other" of the Western woman, finds a point of entry into the hegemonic sphere, in itself enabled by a history of relative cultural and material privilege, she must remember that her speech could be used as representative of a subaltern who is not located within the same sphere of material and cultural privilege. As a participant ethnographer within a South Asian community, it is from a questioning and sometimes hesitant position of authority that I speak. Although this speaking could no doubt be considered as a betrayal on one level, my silence would be a betrayal of another kind.

Continuing my investigation of voice, silence, and representation in online women-centered spaces, I have designed and continue to run various online lists and websites. Ensuring that women are empowered by any kind of technology requires that we investigate issues that are much more complex than merely the question of material access to the latest technologies. The technological practices surrounding the use and design of specific technologies as well as the gendering processes within the communities of production in which these technologies emerged must be examined in detail in order for us to understand the (dis)empowering potential of any particular technology and associated technological practices. Thus, explorations of the gendered subjectivities that emerge within technologically mediated contexts across space, place, and time are necessary if we are to design cyberfeminist technological environments. In the chapters that follow, I discuss my attempts to design and build cyberfeminist webs.

Notes

1. I use the term both in relation to temporal consciousness and epistemological concerns arising from the notion. See Bahri and Vasudeva 1996 for further discussions of the notion of post-colonial/postcolonial.

2. Here I invoke Lisa McLaughlin's definition of "disciplinarity," and "refer to the theories, practices, and institutional arrangements that discriminate among forms of knowledge, specify knowledge and knowledge relationships that coalesce

around 'objects of study,' and demarcate boundaries within which knowledges may take on the appearance of coherence" (1995: 145).

3. Incidentally, to my knowledge, at present any woman can become a member of SAWnet and ask to receive a copy of all past SAWnet digests. Therefore any woman can "verify" that the discussion I am writing about really did occur.

Part Two

BUILDING (SOUTH ASIAN) CYBERFEMINIST WEBS?

CHAPTER FOUR
INTERROGATING IDENTITIES: COMPOSING OTHER CYBERSPACES

Today, with globalization in full swing, telecommunicative informatics taps the Native Informant directly in the name of indigenous knowledge and advances biopiracy.

—Spivak 1999: ix

What (academic, practical, and everyday) discourses and histories are invoked in the juxtaposing of South Asian diasporas and cyberfeminism within the context of a variety of communities of production situated within diverse sociocultural and economic spaciotemporalities? What new utterances might we add in order to disrupt and transform the linear and oppressive teleology of technology, development, and progress discourses? In an effort to find answers to such questions, since 1995 I have been involved with designing and maintaining e-mail discussion spaces and websites concerned with Third-World women's identities.

My theoretical and applied intervention in this area of research and practice began with my dissertation-related work of studying South Asian women online described in part I of this book. This experience led to my building e-spaces in relation to South Asian female subjectivities. In addition to a few scattered websites, my efforts involved starting and maintaining e-mail discussion lists such as Third-World women, women-writing-culture, and sa-cyborgs as a member of the Spoon Collective. My interest in the design of technological environments has also led me to investigate offline real-world locations, including collaborations with Annapurna Mamidipudi, which are discussed in Part III.

I must emphasize that my attempts at designing and building e-spaces are limited to the use of available software and hardware. Since most of this was not designed and put together with the everyday contexts and problems of marginalized populations of the world in mind, my attempts to think through the possible design and use of such technologies in countermainstream ways can only be tactical. My past and current collaborations do not include collaborations with software developers or with hardware designers. Therefore, when I refer to myself as a designer and builder of e-spaces, I am a consumer first of available hardware and technology and, only after that, can I be regarded as a designer and producer of online content. The production aspects with which I am involved include shaping of online spaces such as e-mail lists and websites through discursive (textual) descriptions, setting up the technical features of access for such e-spaces, and the actual designing and building of Web-based interfaces.

In my attempts at designing and building websites and e-mail lists, I have encountered limitations not only in the form of available software and hardware design, but also in the lack of visibility of the socioeconomic and linguistic diversity of populations that access and participate in such contexts classificatory grids situated within Western academic discourse. Labels, definitions, and categories such as gender, race, and class are shaped through discussions and articulations from within a westernized academy and are situated in contexts that are culturally, economically, and historically specific to only certain populations around the world. This means that populations are allowed a voice only within hegemonically available categories and labels. Discourse, itself, however well-intentioned and democratic the rhetoric and ideals contained within it, limits the ability to produce counterspheres.

This chapter is part of a larger discussion of how South Asian diaspora is manifested in the "Intercultural Global Village" (Ess and Sudweeks 2001: 1) in cyberspace (Bahri 2001; Gajjala 1998; Lal 1999b; Mallapragada 2001; Mitra 1997; Rai 1995; Sudha 1993). In an attempt to illustrate the contradictory discourses that emerge online, while discussing the possibilities and impossibilities for opening up counterspheres in cyberspace for alternate collaborative ways of forming communities, I focus on a specific exchange on the sa-cyborgs list. In order to contextualize this exchange, I provide a history of how and why the list was formed.

My examination of South Asian digital diasporas is founded on a basic questioning of the ability of new technologies to further equality. Underlying my analysis is the unavoidable recognition of the fact that the context of intercultural communication in cyberspace is driven through an agenda of commercialization that is implicitly and explicitly digitally Darwinistic, emphasizing the survival of the fastest, as well as the consumption of brand names. As Susan Herring states: "The globalization of the Internet raises intellectual and social challenges concerning cultural bias in CMC, mechanisms of technology diffusion, and barriers to equitable access" (2001: x).

Furthermore, Ess and Sudweeks argue for: "an interdisciplinary effort to explore the role culture plays in forming our fundamental beliefs and values—not only with regard to communication and technology, but still more fundamentally towards such basic values as those that cluster about our preferences for democratic polity, individual autonomy, etc." (2001: 3). They call for: "a distinctive conjunction of theory and praxis—one that articulates interdisciplinary foundations and practical models for designing and using CMC technologies in ways that avoid the Manichean dualism of Jihad or McWorld, and mark out instead a trajectory toward a genuinely intercultural global village" (2001: 4).

While I question the epistemological, political, economic, and cultural premises on which this vision of a "genuinely intercultural global village" implicitly relies, I agree with Ess and Sudweeks regarding the importance of emphasizing the theory and practice of designing, producing, consuming, and interacting in cyberspace. However, I do not agree with what appears to be a positioning of "Jihad" and "McWorld" as two opposites in a Manichean dualism—they are in fact not opposed but products of the same logic of capital and consumption that produces our present postmodern, transnational world. In fact, as Barber suggests, "McWorld cannot do without Jihad . . . neither can Jihad do without McWorld" (Barber 1995: 155). The processes of production and cultural activities surrounding these processes are both products of an economic globalization and transnationalization that rests on the need for self-contained identity formations (consumer demographics) and a performance of multicultural difference. "Jihad" and other religious fundamentalisms and nationalisms (including modern-day "crusades") are examples of "concepts of belonging" and ways of imagining community that are "currently being mobilized in the service of the larger political and economic demands associated with globalization" (Sadowski-Smith 1999: 8).

As is the case with the processes of rebordering and the recent surge of ethnonationalisms in Eastern Europe and elsewhere, different fundamentalisms based in ethnic and religious identity formations are linked to emerging "global reconfigurations" that help the imagining of ethnic and religious communities transnationally while providing selective class-based access to global capital. Thus new hierarchies emerge that feed into "the logic of uneven global development." Sadowski-Smith further states, "It is essential to realize that . . . concepts of belonging are currently being mobilized in the service of larger political and economic demands associated with globalization" (1999: 8).

Situated within such a real-world context, what kind of migratory subjects emerge in digital diaspora[1] at the intersection of the local and the global? What "regulatory fictions" and theoretical frames discipline (in a Foucauldian sense) manifestations of identity formations and communities online? Is communicating as digital diaspora, across contexts, necessarily "empowering"? In this chapter, I examine the (im)possibilities for the emergence of countersubjectivities and counterspheres online[2] with a specific focus on South Asian digital diasporic formations. The emergence of counterspheres and alternate subjectivities (underprivileged or not) requires the opening up of discursive categories (including academic and political reworkings and disruptions of available frameworks). These discursive countercategories allow the imagining of community in different ways (Anderson 1991). By looking at split and conflicted subject positions and the epistemological contradictions and disruptions that emerge through their voicings, scholars might be able to understand how individuals design and produce collaborative counterspheres in cyberspace and elsewhere.

In discussing Chicano as a nationalism, communication scholars Lisa Flores and Marouf Hasian (1997) argue that nationalism is maintained through a sharing of beliefs and symbolic constructs as much as through geographical alliances and communal identities. Adapting Anderson's (1991) notion of imagined communities, they propose a view of nationalism that is constructed through political rhetorics. Flores and Hasian write that nationhood:

is more than a static monolithic concept . . . [and is] a multilayered description of a form that provides us with an "imagined" discursive unit of analysis for studying particular symbol systems. . . . As Anderson once astutely observed, people may believe themselves to be a part of a nation even though they "will never know most of their fellow-members, meet them, or even hear them." . . . These political ties that bind are thus culturally constructed and coproduced by rhetors and their audiences who live in imagined communal relationships. . . . Nationhood can thus be viewed as a rhetorical achievement that may transcend the boundaries of geographic space and historical time. (1997: 189–90)

Such manifestations of imagined nationhood are visible online as diasporic communities come together through virtual meeting spaces such as listservs, bulletin boards, and so on. Digital diasporas of real people form online imagined communities. In this chapter, I focus on South Asian digital diasporas with an emphasis on the imaginings of nationhood that implicitly and explicitly occur along religious frameworks. Thus, several South Asian communities online are framed not along nationalisms based on present geographical boundaries and demographics but on imaginations centered around reproductions of religious discourse in the form of religious diasporas.

It is within such an overall imagined context that the imagining of nationhood in diaspora is framed through various religious fundamentalisms while, at the same time, it is also framed through the discourses of accessing and participating in the transnational corporate world. As Bahri puts it: "Second and third generation South Asians can now connect with those of their own age newly arrived from South Asia (and, of course, with the small but growing number of postcolonies who have access to the internet) to negotiate each other's sense of self " (2001: 224).

South Asians Online

While there is a growing body of mainstream literature on topics related to South Asians and IT (information technology), South Asians in cyberspace, and the digital divide, most of the articles are celebratory with regard to the potential of informational technologies for the various populations of the world. Much of this literature relates to business applications, software production and design for businesses worldwide, and programming, labor, and jobs for South Asians in the rest of the world, or it relates to issues of access of South Asia to the global commercial centers of the world. None of these adequately address the discursive sociocultural spaces that Internet spaces enable, or how the design of information technologies shapes the possibilities and impossibilities of the emergence of marginalized subjectivities.

Perhaps this is so because the discussion in these areas (whether online or offline) does not explicitly engage the sociocultural aspects of technology production, reproduction, and use. Online contributors as well as many scholars of published literature regarding these issues tend to maintain an illusion of secularism and universality and do not confront the basic epistemological problems related to science, technology, and knowledge production being situated within unequal cultural and material power relations.

Other bodies of literature related to South Asia and the IT phenomena do, however, exist. Scholars here examine sociocultural aspects of online activity and discursive formations online in relation to subjectivities that emerge online and to issues such as "voice and voicelessness," "subaltern counterspheres," and so on addressed by cultural studies, postcolonial theory, and feminist theory. Literature examining the sociocultural and communicative aspects of South Asian digital diasporas has been largely done by scholars from a variety of disciplines focusing on the study of South Asia and postcolonialism.

My work draws from this body of literature and connects it with the themes and topics within the field of intercultural communication. Some issues of concern for this latter set of scholars are gender, sexuality, nation and community, construction of South Asian identities in diaspora, subaltern speech, representation of South Asians in Western and global media, and so on. Amit Rai (1995) and Vinay Lal (1999b), for instance, examine the "Hindu diaspora" and the discourses surrounding Hindu-fundamentalist–instigated events in Ayodhya, India, in 1992. As Lal points out in relation to the Indian and South Asian digital diaspora:

> We speak with unreflective ease of the "information revolution," and in this clichéd expression there is the most unambiguous assertion of confidence in the benign telos of history. . . . It is the agenda of the "Internet elites," if they may be so termed, that dictates the modernization and

liberalization of the Indian economy, and it is their interests and ambitions that have led to the emergence of the cell phone culture while the greater part of the country remains without reliable ordinary telephone service. The development of an internationally renowned software industry even while nearly 50 percent of the Indian population remains mired in poverty is yet another of the anomalies engendered by the culture of the Internet elites. Their mobility in cyberspace furnishes them with opportunities to work within the world of international finance and business; like the elites of the First World, they are beginning to live in time, and space poses no barriers for them. . . . The time-space compression that cyberspace typifies only works to the advantage of these elites. (1999b: 137–40)

Others, such as Madhavi Mallapragada (2001), focus on the gendered nature of these online religious diasporas with their implicit and explicit objectification of the Hindu woman as an icon of pure Hindu culture. Mallapragada argues:

The articulation of "Indianness" which is prolific on diasporic websites is problematic for many reasons—chiefly for its idealization of a traditionally uppercaste, middle class male Hindu (oftentimes North Indian Hindu) version of cultural tradition and practices. In the Indian national context, this middle class version of culture achieved and continues to do so, with varying degrees of success, a hegemonic status as Indian culture. This particular dynamic of class, caste, gender, religion, and language continues to be pertinent in diasporic spaces. (2001: 9)

This idealization of a specific type of masculinity relies on the objectification of an Indian and Hindu femininity. Rai (1995), for instance, addresses the gendered nature of these online diasporas by pointing out how these discourses engage the history of the Indian nationalist resolution of the "Woman's Question," which objectified the woman as an icon of cultural purity, the maintainer of the cultural essence of home. An image of the "New Hindu woman" was produced in such nationalistic discourses. This woman was the "other" of the common woman, who was "coarse, vulgar, loud, quarrelsome, devoid of superior moral sense, and sexually promiscuous" (Chatterjee 1989: 238–39). The construction of such a woman in nationalist discourses carried into the diasporic means that South Asian women in diaspora face a double bind in relation to the

Western feminism and resistance to colonial discourses sometimes implicit in liberal feminist attempts to "save" the "oppressed" Third-World woman. Western feminist narratives regarding Third-World women seem to echo colonial discourses (only in this case, instead of the white man attempting to rescue the brown woman from the brown man, it is a case of the white woman trying to "enlighten" the "politically immature" brown woman). Indian and other South Asian feminists are faced with a problem in relation to their national identities. Feminism is equated with "westernization," and femininity is equated with the traditional and objectified female in nationalist discourse. Online, therefore, the South Asian woman is faced with negotiating the gendered nature of South Asian digital diasporas and the implicit class-based, colonial hierarchies and rules and "regulatory fictions" (Butler, cited in Rai 1995: 33) that police online interaction (such as "netiquette").

Rai (1995) examines the style in which online diasporic communities are imagined and notes that imagined communities of South Asians in digital diaspora are shaped through the "regulatory fictions" produced by officers of the British Empire. For instance, it is such classificatory grids (such as the census categories and definitions of gender identity, caste, and religion based on the British social understandings and framings of "Indian" social structures), categories produced under British rule, that became "the antagonisms that constituted what came to be known as 'representative' communal politics under the British Raj" (Rai 1995: 37). These classificatory grids continue to shape and frame discourse even within online spaces populated mostly by Western-educated elite populations. Thus, the effect of the circulation of such grids continues to result in the reproduction of the same tensions and ideologies that are visible within diasporic communities not online (the communities in real life). Rai, therefore, does not see such online spaces as "oppositional" formations in the sense suggested by those that talk about the radical democratizing potential of cyberspace. It is thus through the "totalizing classificatory grid[s]" (Anderson 1991: 184) produced in British colonial times that South Asian identities—in the form of communal and religious diasporas—are performed online. These classificatory grids have been further extended to work within a multicultural global(ized) village. The performance of diasporic identities in these online communities is thus regulated and mediated through historic, political, and religious discourses associated with colonial and postcolonial geographic territories and nationalisms.

Furthermore, the South Asian digital diaspora exists between the notions of "being home" and "being away." Even while many from actual Third-World geographical (home) locations are connected and online, the discourse is framed by notions of being home and being away; not having left home yet (or at all) and having arrived (i.e., made it) in the Western world.[3] These discourses are situated in themes of nostalgia and reconstructions of South Asian immigrant identities invoked in contexts of diaspora and travel shaped by transnational capital and labor flow. Thus they are continually negotiating "model minority" performances and essentialized cultural performances based on fetishized, mummified notions of "home" traditions and cultural practices. These multicultural cyborgs, visible in digital diasporic contexts, therefore exist in an ethos of continual reconfiguration and shifting of narratives in relation to being home and being away, while simultaneously they are also about not having left home yet and having arrived. These various reconfigurations do not occur "through the heroic act of an individual (the migrant), but through the forming of [virtual] communities that create multiple identifications through collective acts of remembering in the absence of a shared knowledge or a familiar terrain" (Ahmed 1999: 329). They occur through collective acts of storytelling and sharing of knowledge and experience of the "unfamiliar" and "new" terrains.

Some of these self-narratives by model native informants, who have moved "away" from home, yet fetishized "home" while celebrating their moving away and arriving as progressive (social upward mobility), perform the dual and simultaneous function of "modernization" and "exoticization" of the postcolonial (underdeveloped) subject.[4]

It is against such a South Asian technospatial imaginary that sa-cyborgs was started. Sa-cyborgs[5] is an e-mail list, born out of my dilemmas in relation to the above, started with the idea of trying to experiment against, examine, and negotiate such frameworks within the ethos of cyberspace.

Sa-cyborgs

In an attempt to illustrate the contradictory discourses that emerge online, I focus on an exchange between M, G, T, and R[6] on the sa-cyborgs list. In

53

order to contextualize this exchange, I provide a history of how and why the list was formed. Note, however, that neither the interaction nor the e-mail discussion list should be considered "representative" in any sense.

My experience within a women-only South Asian e-mail discussion list (SAWnet) during summer 1995 (see Gajjala 1998, 2002) led me to ask questions regarding the design and production aspect of interactive Internet spaces such as e-mail discussion lists. In an effort to understand the technical and applied process of founding and maintaining a discussion list focused on women and creative expression, I started e-mail discussion lists (specifically the Third-World women list, women-writing-culture list, and sa-cyborgs, which originated as seminar-13) with the help of the Spoon Collective. Prior to starting these lists, I gained experience moderating e-mail lists by being one of several moderators for the discussion list SAWnet and comoderating the postcolonial list as a member of the Spoon Collective. Over the years, the sa-cyborgs policies and list description have been changed periodically based on the problems encountered and conflicts that have occurred. These changes can be viewed in the public Web archives of the list from http://lists.village.virginia.edu/~spoons. The latest information sheet describes the list as follows:

> This list focuses on interactive, experimental creative writing with an implicit focus on gender, race, class, caste, sexuality, age, geographical location . . .
>
> identity/political/economic/spacio-temporal/geographic . . . issues pertaining to voice and voicelessness, silence and resistance, Self and Other narratives . . .
>
> "women" produce "writerly texts" (writerly texts—see Barthes—interrupt conventions of reading/writing and require readers to participate in meaning making—online this can happen visibly only if you participate on-list . . . "readerly texts," on the other hand, are those which fulfill our expectations of conventions that allow readers to be passive consumers . . . this is not the goal of this "list"). Participation is thus necessary and invited. Note that the focus is on "wo-men's" subjectivities and creative "self" writing. Also note that there are implicit rules for list users that are not articulated in the info sheet. There are a variety of theoretical and practical reasons for these implicit rules, as well as for the explicit rules. (See the archives at http://lists.village .virginia.edu/~spoons for more on these rules[7]).

The information sheet continues:

> Rude, sexist, racist, classist and so on interruptions will not be tolerated. Join with an open adventurous mind. Don't expect to understand it all. There are no organized dictionaries for the unsaid, yet-to-be-said, the silences and refusals of counter-hegemonic narratives . . . nor should there be.

In framing and reframing the sa-cyborgs list, I have not only confronted the limitations of the available populations of cyberspace but also faced the limitations of westernized academic categories for analysis based on the assumptions implicit in available categories such as gender, race, subaltern, and so on. Just as the classificatory grids from the British Raj time continue to be reproduced within and constrain bourgeois online diasporic spaces (Rai 1995), classificatory grids situated within Western academic discourse have imposed limitations that affect how I open up online spaces for discussion. Thus, even labels, definitions, and categories such as gender, race, and class are shaped through discussions and articulations from within a westernized academy and are situated in contexts that are culturally, economically, and historically specific to only certain populations around the world. They therefore impose ways of seeing that close off options for speaking by the people living within the contexts that the academics and policy makers are describing. This means that the populations that seek a voice are allowed a voice only within hegemonically available categories and labels. Discourse (however well intentioned and democratic the rhetoric and ideals contained within it) becomes limiting to the ability to produce counterspheres. These struggles for articulation are visible in the archives of sa-cyborgs.

Performing Diasporic Identity Locations[8]

Based on their posts to the list, M and G have been members of the list since 1996. Lacking face-to-face contact with either of these people, I cannot claim to know that either of these women is definitely South Asian or even that they are indeed women. In the case of one of them, however, I have talked with her by telephone, exchanged personal e-mails, as well as engaged with her on other e-mail discussion lists; I am quite sure that she is a South Asian woman who has lived in the United States for a considerable number of years. In the case of the other individual, I have guessed that she has some connection to "South Asianness" based on her posts to the lists. I have also seen her name appear on conference panels. Both women have contributed creative work to the sa-cyborgs list, and their writing has sometimes been centered on identity negotiations based in postcolonial female subjectivities. I have no real information on who T is, except that she is at a university in New York. I have been active since the list was started. My own multiply mediated sociocultural locations are variously visible through http://www.cyberdiva.org. While posts by T and R are used in my analyses in this chapter, below I focus on the exchange between G and M. A complex, layered history is apparent in G's subject position, as expressed by her in the following piece of writing posted to the list in October 1996:[9]

Afrindianativeamaboriginalausinuitquechuafilmmaking
I screen/teach
and I read white
ethnograppleanthroapologetical
white/black breasted nation algeographic
gazeye knowledgeablepower
and the whiteaustralianboy drugged out sleeps on the leather tutorial seat
saying I didn't get up today because nothing came up about
whiteheterosexualmales
faces that read
whileIgoonandonaboutracegenderandclassandthebolivianswhoweresteri
lizedbythebadassedpeacecorpsortheamericanswhohelpedmassacrepe
asantsinsouthamerica
my skin
oncetheylearnedabouttheuniversalityoftheirartandtheirknowledgeandthe
irmight
brown a sign
whichstillradiateslikeawhitehotspearthroughthefleshofthosethatliveandd
ieinthis
theageofneocolonialgrandeur
that I speak
butnowtheytireoflearningaboutculturaldifferenceandminorityoppressedg
roups
toomuchworktheysayandwhydowehavetolearnhistoriesofdarknessandstr

uggle
but will not be heard
abovetheroarof theirmy word
"Those epistemologicaterminal terms dammit"

The present discussion will be based on one specific interaction between G and M, about M's writing. This piece of writing authored by M
was posted to the list by me in October 1999, with M's permission from
the South Asian Women's Forum website, and it is available in full at
http://www.sawf.org/newedit/edit101899/index.asp.

ABHIMAAN
Yesterday's India,
I remember you.
Inexplicable, daunting exile
clutches at culture not mine.
Inner flashes grope for meaning:
Three blind men define Elephant.
The edges of my mind
flanked by Hindu myths
grasp life-shaping images.
Devout Prahlad cannot save an Unbeliever
devoured by a raging, ravaging Lion
God's alter ego fastens its teeth
tearing at flesh.
The Unbeliever is Prahlad's father.
The disciple cobra refuses to even hiss
and bleedingly succumbs to stones and rocks
and his guru's musing
"Yes, remain nonviolent, but surely
you can stand up for your rights?"
Hinduism molds me.
I question what I see,
hasten after what I cannot.
I defer to greatness reduced to ashes.
Desperate pounding rhythms
distanced from days filled
with anguished cries caught

between reality and dreams
give no succor to the heart.
Heart beats rival
perilous rhythms,
desolate measures
of silent depths.

As we can see, both these creative pieces are expressions of negotiations of gendered diasporic subjectivities. Each of the authors in her own way was struggling with available categories and labels and to identify and disidentify with available categories of belonging and owning and disowning of several histories based on the displacements and dislocations experienced by each. Each of these pieces, in its own way, performs an "outside the sentence[ness]" (Bhabha 1994: 180).[10]

Exchanges on the list create problematic spaces of the sort described by Barthes (1975) and Bhabha (1994: 180–82) in relation to various South Asian diasporic imaginings of community available online and carry the possibility to open up "narrative strateg[ies] for the emergence and negotiation of those agencies of the marginal, minority, subaltern, or diasporic that incite us to think through—and beyond—theory" (Bhabha 1994: 181).

While G's form in writing seems to indicate a problematization of the very structure and form of meaning making available to her, as her words and sentences run into each other and emotions and thoughts leak in and out of given categories, M's form in writing suggests a more conventional (but "conventional" only in comparison to G's writing) negotiation of available structures for self-expression. Yet neither is writing traditional English poetry in any sense. It is obvious that in writing they both seek tactics for disrupting available frameworks that do not allow for the emergence of complex, contradictory subjectivities with multiple, layered histories of travel and continually mutating cultural practices.

G's entry reflects a struggle with layers of regulatory fictions shaped by colonial placements of race, patriarchal positioning of gender, teleological narratives of progress, and the universalizing of westernized epistemologies, as they regulate her students' ability to hear her voice as she speaks. M writes apparently from within, yet problematizes British colonial regulatory fictions of the "Hindu" imaginary. She slips outside of these frames; in her retelling of mythology and stories from the Upanishads and Panchatantras, and the invoking of Shiva's ashes (all unified under the term "Hindu"), she fleetingly, if hesitantly, dares to touch on the unbeliever's view, she refuses the homogeneity imposed on so-called Hinduism by British colonial and Indian nationalistic regulatory frames.

For instance, she apparently aligns her view with that in colonial descriptions of the Indian woman by writing "Hinduism molds me," but she quickly switches from an implicit tone of cultural and religious piety to a tone that goes against the grain of the perception of non-Christian religions that colonial descriptions encourage with the next sentence, "I question what I see/ hasten after what I cannot," thus defiantly characterizing Hinduism as a culture that encourages the questioning of authority.

The exchanges that happened between October 18, 1999, and October 22, 1999, on the sa-cyborgs list[11] construct a problematic, discursive social space. There is something in M's self-explanation of the writing of this poem (placed next to the poem at http://www.sawf.org/newedit/edit101899/index.asp) that appears to invoke conventionally available imagining of Indianness through regulatory frameworks situated in a colonial discourse that constructs "America" as new. The following section of the explanation, for instance, seems to romanticize a past through a colonial and/or modernist imaginary that juxtaposes the "ancient" of India with the "new" of America:

> G (to M): While your poem is perhaps intense for you, it really breaks my heart to see how our (Indian immigrant) poeticizing (if I can coin that word) reinstalls a colonial repetitiveness in the affirmation of the United States as "new world." Turtle Island, one of the U.S.'s many names, was only new to those who came from Europe. There are never "new worlds" or frontiers, not even in space.

M and G on Poetries and Histories

I refer mainly to the thread entitled "poetries and histories" next. In this exchange, the continuity of emotion (in this case, nostalgia for an imagined or remembered homeland and coming to terms with a certain self-identity as an immigrant Indian) invoked in the poem by M and the commentary that follows is disrupted (discontinued) by G's apparently sudden question, which displaces the perhaps intended (expected, anticipated) narrative logic of the poet. In this exchange, G insists on disidentifying herself from the "weness" implicit in M's narrative, while noting "how our (Indian immigrant) poeticizing reinstalls a colonial repetitiveness in the affirmation of the United States as 'new world.'"

In addition—after some more list exchanges—G clarifies that it was not the poem itself that was the sole cause of her reaction:

> G: Perhaps there are other things we need to ask ourselves here. Why is it that we "feel" like foreigners? Isn't it because the systems of racism and colonization that resulted in the dispossession of Native Americans continue to extend to other groups even if they are "born" in this land. I mean just think of the absurdity of people who belong to this land having to struggle to survive emotionally, psychically, politically, physiologically, let alone survive economically.
>
> In this sense, I'm not attacking you, I just think we need to understand these histories and the connections between them in a way that is anticolonial, otherwise we are dictated by the very language we communicate in even as we feel the conditions of exile in whatever manifestation it may be.

Even as M's moving poem invokes affective identification points for many immigrant Indians, and suggests a metaphoric representation of Indian immigrants' feeling "othered" yet at home in the United States, the comments inserted in the discussion contrast with a unitary reading of the exchange within the technospatial South Asian imaginary.

While the exchange itself does not lead to a dialogue or a "resolution" of conflict, it holds the possibility of leading to associations "based on contiguity and context" (Jarratt 1998: 59). As M points out, the way the poem was read was not how she intended it to be read. The decoding (meaning-making) processes surrounding the reading of the poem did not result in the meaning she intended to encode. In the following posts, she explains her intention, which in fact turns out not to be opposed to G's critique. G and M, it appears, were using different experiential and theoretical lenses.

> M: By "new world," I mean it can never have a rich history. If I'm politicizing, then I'm politicizing the fact that as a citizen of this nation, I still have felt an exile, thanks to 10 job losses within 3 decades. America does

not, still, welcome "foreigners." We are second-class citizens. Thus, my feeling like an "exile." It *is*[12] political, regardless of the academic and philosophic argument we could have over semantics. If I cannot survive economically, then what is America but "new" to me. And I actually grew up here, had all my schooling [here] since [I was] a child of seven.

I am not politicizing anything, but have been politicized by a country I thought I belonged in from childhood, but as an adult realized I do not, and felt the pangs of an "exile," forgotten by the country of my birth.

Why is America "new" to me . . . again, it is an experiment in living on land and space belonging . . . to others. It is Eurocentric, perhaps the worst example of that, and its institutions do not take to criticism well, if at all.

G: These comments are not meant to be harsh, please take it in the spirit of dialogue. My heart didn't break because of your poem, it breaks when I realize how much "we" still need to decolonize ourselves. I never said you were politicizing, I said you were poeticizing and, in doing that, affirming a colonial narration of the U.S. Perhaps that is a productive misreading.

M: I agree with you. My essay is a glimpse what America has been for me politically, economically, and emotionally . . . a total drain on my energy.

I'm aware that Massachusetts has its own Native Americans who are searching for their identity and their land, and have been rewarded with casinos. By "new world" I meant that America is "new" because it is the history of Europe extended to North America, displacing indigenous peoples. And still an experiment, one that seems to have failed every other people except those of European descent. And how can it have been otherwise? With our Eurocentric educations, generations of us have fallen into the expected and predictable grooves.

I also agree with you about language. As long as we communicate using the language of colonizers, we won't reach an "anticolonial" solution. Also, I don't feel that being "anti-" anything can help us. We have to revive who we are. The parables in my poem are a definition of who I really am. As for the histories of all of us and our connections, that's existing knowledge; in fact, that's knowledge that has existed for millennia, but the U.S., especially, has left our roots behind in the dust. Those of us who value those roots can revive them but that revival has no ground to stand on. We either conform per expectation, as stereotypes, or we die. An exile's longing for those roots never dies. Perhaps it's time to find a language in which to communicate.

G: See, I'm still not sure we're in on the same force field (if I can put it that way). Any "we" is always defined in relation to the other "we" are defining against. In this case, the "we" is getting defined against an America that is identified with Europe as you say. As we know, America in terms of populations and identities is not another Europe. There are specific reasons for displacements and migrations for the different group identities. Also, maybe it is time to take into account the whole plant, not just roots. The becoming that iswaswillbe which will not either conform to stereotypes or die.

I say this also because I question the weness, the oneness of words like India, statehoods which in themselves like the naming of America or U.S. become grounds for erasures of histories, poetries in other ways.

M: "We" can go round and round with this and nothing will ever change. India was never a nation. Understood. Neither was America. Understood. I wrote a poem about my feeling like an exile in a country that is supposed to be my home. Let's just leave it that. I fairly tire of academic debates which lead nowhere. If you and R want to do a semantic analysis, please go ahead, without me! :) We all know all of the things you and R mention. The point is, everyday people still field the arrows of stereotype regardless of how the argument is phrased academically regarding "we" and "nationhood," postcolonial fallout notwithstanding.

"Contrary to the assumptions that brought some of us to the United States, we may thus find ourselves forced to contend with our places of departure, asked to function as native informants from 'elsewhere.' From what position of authority would we speak? The very attempt to become such cultural representatives, the falterings of our memory, must, then, lead to a different realization: the need for an examination of the historical, institutional, and social relations that have, in fact, produced subjects so quite unlike 'the native informant' of old" (John 1996: 26).

Posts on Intentionality and Reading— Intersecting Threads

R: What we perceive as "my" meaning "my intentions" often work with existing narrations and discourses to reproduce hierarchies—even unintentionally—what you term "mis/interpretation mis/representation" happen based on varied con/texts of reading and varied (multiple) con/texts of writing and meaning thus not even the "original author" has absolute control (authority) over her/his meaning—there is always a surplus that gets picked up.

M: Every writer has ownership over intent. If that intent gets changed through whatever other action, then it is no longer the original writer's "words" nor is the original writer the owner of that changed meaning. What happened on this list, I feel, is a politicization of my writing which was not my intent. My intent was and is self awareness and re-definition out of any hierarchy. Academic language shrouds reality like no other use of language can! If we want to emerge from power structures and hierarchies, perhaps we should begin by shunning the language of those entities. However, as academics, I find we merely serve to recycle the same through generations.

M: I have no issue with the "borrowing, re-using, spitting out and circulating," etc. I have an issue with jumping to erroneous conclusions never intended by the writer and then interminable rhetoric over such presumptions. Of course words travel . . . whatever their form . . . This has been true from the first recorded word(s), but does not in any way exonerate misrepresentation, misinterpretation, lack of understanding (vs. misunderstanding).

T:thissuddenrushedswirloftangledintentsstruckmeassalienttheFirsttimearoundbutcaughtinthelensoftranslationinthetransitsofinterpretationthemessagechangessometimes.sometimesforthebetterandsometimesforworseandsometimesjustchangesthatonethingissure.doesanyonehearderridatalkinthedistanceofthisconversation?derridatalksofmorphologyofgrammatologysofaccentsandglyphs.derridasaysnotmuchnewnothingthatthoseonthislisthavenotalreadysaid.hetalksofthewaysthat"meanings"travelthroughtimeandtraverse.transitthroughtimeandthroughspacemeansanticipatethemultiplewaysinwhichothersuntieones"own"senseandmakenew.alwaysanticipatesandwiches:thesinewylayersofnostalgiaamnesiadistortionrepressionandpersonalmemorythatreaderswillbringto"ones"texts.alwaysanticipateghosts.intentionisnotsomethingstableorfixedbutratherasnakeinthegrassaspringajackintheboxan"abracadabra"anewsongnewsoundsofullofdistortion,yetthere.anoldsonganoldsoundandoldhold, stillthere.

"Agreedisagreeagreedisagreedisagreeagreemymindisnowinaswirl ofbinaryframingididnotintendbutwhathasagreedisagreegottodowiththeissuesathandiwonderwhatmyintentreally isdoyouknowperhaps?"

These writers struggle with layers of regulatory fictions and personal histories, as well as identifications and disidentifications that might enable an exchange to produce a community that allows an imagining outside of these frames. In this chapter, I have attempted to explore these issues, through a focus on a set of interpersonal exchanges that occurred in a public space (a publicly archived e-mail discussion list). Such interpersonal exchanges are obviously not unique to "the Internet" spaces—such debates and conversations occur often in everyday life. Nor are they totally enabled by the technology. However, cyberspace is relevant to this exchange because it is situated in a South Asian digital diaspora enabled by the Internet. These spaces have become sites for the emergence of South Asian diasporic connections, and it is important to examine how they are being framed and how they permit certain voicings.

Furthermore, as Gurak points out:

> It is important to move away from generalizations about life in cyberspace and begin to analyze specific instances of computer-mediated-communication, not only as a way of understanding patterns of current discourse but also as a method of building theory so we can design communication systems that encourage new social spaces that are appropriate, functional, accessible, and, perhaps even democratic. (1997: ix)

In addition to being cautious and aware of the celebratory technospatial imaginary and mainstream discourses regarding information technologies and the Internet as great equalizers, it is important for us to reexamine our assumptions and look for possibilities for alternate uses of this medium, rather than totally discounting them in dystopic reaction. It is important to examine the populations using this medium and discourses they build together.

Notes

1. The word "diaspora" can be traced back to the notion of the Jewish diaspora and suggests the idea of dispersal and fragmentation; and in much of the literature there is a presumed relationship between the diasporic community and the land that they left and to which the possibility of return always subsists, or what we are apt to term "motherland" or "home." The conditions that make for diasporic community are admittedly complex, but this presumed link between the diasporic community and the motherland is easily questioned, nor is there any

reason why we must be held hostage to any linguistic and epistemological tyranny. No substantive issue can be decided on the issue of "origins." It thus appears perfectly reasonable to speak of an Indian Diaspora, as it does of the Chinese Diaspora, the African Diaspora, the Palestinian Diaspora, and of course, the Jewish Diaspora (Lal 1999a: 42). By "digital diaspora" I simply mean various traveling transnational subjectivities that inhabit online spaces.

2. I use the terms to mark oppositional, marginalized, and alternative subjectivities (countersubjectivities) and the social spaces composed through the interaction of such subjectivities (counterspheres) drawing from Nancy Fraser's critique and rearticulation of the Habermasian public sphere, where she maps a topology of opposition and fractures the paradigm of the public sphere. Fraser argues that instead of "the" public sphere, we must speak of numerous counterspheres (i.e., many social spaces of discussion embedded within circuits of unequal power). She asserts that "public life in egalitarian, multi-cultural societies cannot consist exclusively in a singe, overarching lens" (Fraser 1990: 59). Countersubjectivities therefore are subjectivities that if performed would fracture the apparent homogeneity of "the" public opinion in any social space.

3. See, for instance, online spaces such as www.rediff.com.

4. Such discourses and self-narratives can be viewed over the Internet—look especially in recent discussions concerning the Hijab and Muslim women. See http://newsvote.bbc.co.uk/hi/English/talking_point/debates/south_asian/newsid _1530000/15302stm, where some posts fall into this category.

5. See http://lists.village.virginia.edu/~spoons.

6. M, G, and T gave me permission to cite from their online interactions on the list. R is me. It should also be noted that sa-cyborgs is a publicly archived list.

7. These rules are based on my experiences online since 1994, which I can cite. Feel free to discuss these with me "off-list" sometime.

8. M and G are published poets and scholars and their work is available in public spaces. Their full names are available in the archives of sa-cyborgs and elsewhere on the Internet. T has remained anonymous.

9. To get a better idea of the form that G used in her post, please refer to this URL: http://lists.village.virginia.edu/~spoons and search the archives for the posts in October 1996 under the thread "poetry and histories."

10. "Outside the sentence[ness]," as I use it, is articulated in Homi Bhabha's essay "The Postcolonial and the Postmodern" (Bhabha 1994: 171–97), where he also uses the phrase "beyond theory." In an effort to evoke the notion of "a liminal form of signification that creates space for the contingent," which he refers to as being "beyond theory," he draws from Roland Barthes's "exploration of the cultural space 'outside the sentence'" (Bhabha 1994: 179).

11. This chapter contains a very small portion of the whole exchange, which can be found in the archives of sa-cyborgs at http://lists.village.virginia.edu/~spoons.

12. Placing an * on either side of a word, phrase, or sentence is an e-mail convention used (like italics) to show emphasis.

CHAPTER FIVE
BUILDING CYBERFEMINIST WEBS

In an exploration of possibilities for building e-spaces for the empowerment of women, I am faced with issues similar to those faced by many feminist activists and scholars who have begun to articulate the impossibility of isolating "Woman" as a category that is often based in implicit assumptions regarding a universalized dual gender system, which in reality is situated in particular sociocultural and economic locations. As Linda Alcoff and Elizabeth Potter point out, therefore:

> Growing awareness of the many ways in which political relationships (that is, disparate power relations) are implicated in theories of knowledge has led to the conclusion that gender hierarchies are not the only ones that influence the production of knowledge. Cognitive authority is usually associated with a cluster of markings that involve not only gender but also race, class, sexuality, culture, [geographical location, caste, language], and age. Moreover, developments in feminist theory have demonstrated that gender as a category of analysis cannot be abstracted from a particular context while other factors are held stable; gender can never be observed as a "pure" or solitary influence. Gender identity cannot be adequately understood—or even perceived—except as a component of complex interrelationships with other systems of identification and hierarchy. (1993: 3)

Further, as has been argued by postcolonial theorists, universalizing categories without regard to context is a colonizing act in and of itself (Bhabha 1994).

In exploring questions related to gender and technology, therefore, I complicate them with issues concerning class, race, caste, geographical location, and cultural histories in an attempt to understand constructs of identity and ignorance that shape access to and empowerment through various technologies.

The case studies discussed in this chapter raise questions such as: What might "women-centered" practices of ICT design and use look like? Do women-centered strategies necessarily allow entry to women from all backgrounds irrespective of race, class, caste, sexuality, and geographic location? How would egalitarian women-friendly technological environments be structured? Is it possible to develop cyberfeminist strategies for the development of technological environments and practices that will be empowering for various marginalized populations of the world? Are available conceptual grids and categories for defining and conceptualizing marginalized populations and their needs useful for such a project?

The overall body of research that this chapter draws on for its theoretical framework questions "the specific cultural setting and world view that gives significance to these practices from the point of view of the bequeathers" (Marvin 1988: 14). It is argued that some of these specific cultural settings in which the design of technologies are situated can be at odds with the worldviews and everyday practices within the sociocultural communities that we are attempting to empower and bequeath (see for instance Shiva 1994). My approach to finding solutions, therefore, emphasizes the redesigning of "new" technological environments, rather than a mere attempt at "transferring" so-called advanced technologies in the name of a notion of "Progress" that is in itself situated in socioeconomic, historical, and political contexts not necessarily empowering to all communities of the world (Markley 1996). Technological environments are social environments shaped around the use of any type of "technology." Such social environments are place-based and their structuring is shaped by local histories, geographical conditions, and everyday cultural practices within which specific technologies are put to use. It is important to emphasize the unequal power relations within which all the factors that shape such environments coexist.

The relationship between processes of gendering in everyday life and the ways in which such gendering shapes technology design as well as the environments surrounding their use is emphasized. Therefore it is suggested that research closely examine multiple mediated contexts of technology design and use, as a model for understanding the scope for empowerment of women through information communication technologies. Empowerment for women within technological environments would mean that they would have better access to the power structures and hierarchies that shape and control such environments. They would in fact have the power (implicit and explicit) to shape these environments in such a way as to make them inviting to diverse populations.

Experiences within a women-only south Asian e-mail discussion list (SAWnet) in summer 1995 (see chapters 1, 2, and 3) led to current and ongoing research regarding the design and production aspect of interactive Internet spaces such as e-mail discussion lists. Efforts to understand the technical and applied process of founding and maintaining a discussion list focused on women and creative expression led to the formation of some e-mail discussion lists (specifically the Third-World women list, women-writing-culture list, and sa-cyborgs) with the help of the Spoon Collective.[1] A central question behind these attempts was: Is it possible for women to find electronic space as a site for reinventing and re-representing themselves or have the more traditional representations and structures of femininity— both textual and visual—found in mass culture simply found a new home in a new medium, leaving women both complicit and resistant to the more dominant, less subversive image of Woman within mass culture?

Claims in this section are based on experiences of founding, moderating, and shaping the Third-World women list and women-writing-culture list (both now often silent) and the continual framing and reframing of the sa-cyborgs list. Contradictions emerged within these spaces even as the attempt was to frame them as e-spaces that would be enabling for dialogue and cooperation.

The Third-World women list was founded in fall 1995 from my University of Pittsburgh e-mail account as "Representing"[2] and then moved to the Spoon Collective with the name of Third-World women. On this list, as is apparent by the name, we would be discussing issues related to women of the Third World from various interdisciplinary, academic, and nonacademic perspectives. The women-writing-culture list was started in June 1996. This list was to focus more generally on issues related to women, writing, and culture in relation to the dilemmas faced by feminist ethnographers and anthropologists.

The following two claims are based on experiences with these lists:

1. The exclusions implicit in the universalizing of the notion of a so-called women's way of communicating within women-centered online contexts sometimes succeeds in silencing "Other" women and could lead to outbursts of what is perceived as flaming.

2. An examination of the subject that emerges in the interstices of flaming and lurking, within so-called woman-centered online discussion contexts, could lead to a better understanding of the sociocultural as well as political and economic framing of social spaces online.

The clusters of interaction that I look at in relation to the above two claims come from the women-writing-culture list and the Third-World women list. Each of these lists has a list culture co-constructed by the various participant members, as well as nonparticipant members of the lists (based on the argument that silence shapes discourse).[3]

The clusters were chosen based on the fact that their content helps illustrate how the above stated claims are relevant within the contexts of these lists. The ongoing sets of interactions are available in the public archives of the two lists and are linked to the Spoon Collective website at http://lists.village.virginia.edu/~spoons.

Women-writing-culture: Universalizing a Situated Women's Way of Communicating/Knowing?

Examining the initial clusters of interaction on women-writing-culture, it becomes apparent that members set up a pattern of interaction that is clearly based on what Herring (1996) has identified as women's posting styles. Women and even some of the men sending out posts to the list adopted supportive styles of posting and maintained a level of respect for each other that is not the norm in a majority of e-spaces. This can be evidenced by an examination of the thread on "shall we have some brief intros for starters?" (started July 23, 1996), for example. For the most part, during the following weeks, months, and even years (right until December 1998 when I shut down the list), conversations on the list were some-times continuous and sometimes sporadic.

Posts tended to be generally friendly, very patient, and tolerant, but not so tolerant of what some members might perceive as contentious responses. On this list, I was more often a lurker-moderator/technician than an actively participating moderator/technician. As time pro-gressed, a group of women and men on the list seemed to have formed a pleasant, cozy group of virtual friends and seemed to have formed an interesting "caucus" of their own in relation to the general list title of "women-writing-culture."

The moderating style on women-writing-culture for the most part was nonintrusive and no active effort was made to direct conversations so that they explicitly tied back to what the information sheet promised members when they joined the list. Some of us were lulled into a sense of nonconfrontational "sisterhood" and felt happy to occasionally contribute a creative piece related to the list focus or just insert a comment or two into conversations every now and then. There was a self-conscious at-tempt to avoid asserting online moderator authority in what is often termed a "male" style. In an attempt to create a woman-centered e-space, then, I was actually being a passive moderator allowing an "anything goes" attitude in the name of the women-writing-culture situation.

However, as it turned out, the lack of assertion of any kind of author-ity on my part created problems for the maintaining of list focus in the long run. Some members began to see posts by the vocal members, who (sometimes "chattily") exchanged personal stories on-list, as being irrele-vant to the list focus. Around the end of 1998, however, a few new mem-bers who had joined based on what the information sheet described the list to be, as well as some older member-lurkers on the list, began to make their restlessness apparent via back-channel communication with me, the moderator of the list. A few women expressed their opinion that they felt they had no point of entry into the discussions, in addition to which, a couple of others wondered what the present discussion on the list had to do with what the information sheet promised.

Part of the problem of asserting authority in women-centered spaces that get defined as "nurturing," "supportive," and so on is that authorita-tive statements and an emphasis on rules risks being associated with male modes of articulation. "[N]orms and rules" that need to be articulated are associated with male values that "generally have excluded females and values associated with the feminine" (Jones 1988: 119). Therefore, asserting authority as moderator and cutting short some exchanges on the list would have alienated me from some very nice, gentle women who were actively participating on the list. Kathleen B. Jones argues that the "very definition of authority as a set of practices designed to institutionalize social hierarchies lies at the root of the separation of women qua women from the process of 'authorizing'" (1988: 120). As Jones further suggests,

> If . . . the dichotomy between compassion and authority contributes to the association of the authoritative with a male voice, then the implication is that the segregation of women and the feminine from authority is internally connected to the concept of authority itself. (1988: 120)

Assertion of authority in women-centered spaces thus becomes problematic and conflictive.

In the case of women-writing-culture, it appears that, although the list space was a very pleasant place to be, it was not accomplishing the complexity of dialogue that such an e-space with its global intersections and connections might potentially accomplish. Women who were outside of the popular and everyday culture that the friendly caucus online had begun to share did not feel free to interrupt and assert their opinions and presence. Being nonadversarial and supportive on this list came to mean[4] that participants could not express their dissent outside of the essentialist "women's way" framing of discourse on-list. In such a situation, for some lurkers who came from RL (i.e., "Real Life") contexts that were very different from the active participants' RL contexts, to "delurk" might mean appearing jarring and intrusive on the list.

Third-world-women: Contentiousness May Lead to Dialogue (or Not)?

In contrast to the women-writing-culture situation,[5] an examination of some clusters of exchange on the Third-World women list reveals that contentiousness can sometimes lead to dialogue, even if the dialogue is not always visible online (i.e., the dialogue and collaborations between members may also happen off-list, in what is sometimes referred to as "back-channel" communication). It is also worth noting that, although discussions got heated at times, I did not need to actively intervene as moderator to "control" participants' behavior online. At that time in the history of the list, they did a fairly good job of countering each others' arguments in ways that were productive enough to allow dialogue.

My speculation is based on sites of conflict/contradiction/contention in various clusters of interaction on the Third-World women list as well as other lists that I have ever lurked on or actively participated on. In the present discussion, my observation is based directly on an examination of two main clusters of interaction on the Third-World women list and indirectly on my general experience online for the past eight years.

These clusters of exchanges occurred in October and November 1998. In these interactions, the subjects that emerged were men and women struggling with and against hegemonic framing of controversial topics related to women originally from non-Western nations and in fact the second cluster can be seen as continuing to exchange with some of the same conflicts and issues in relation to patriarchy, Western feminism, and women from Third-World contexts that the first exchange was concerned with.

The cluster of exchanges that started on October 2, 1998, was mainly about the controversial topic of the Bangladeshi writer Tasleema Nasreen. The discussion touched on sensitive issues related to religion, westernization, and elite women from Third-World nations who speak for or appropriate the status of the oppressed "Other" in ways that are complicit with colonial discourses about the Third-World "Other." The cluster of exchanges that started on October 31, 1998, was triggered by an announcement regarding a conference on dowry and bride-burning in India. Both issues are highly complicated and sensitive topics for women from non-Western areas of the world and for women who have emotional, religious, and cultural ties to the non-Western world. Both issues revolve around the positioning of "woman" within Western and non-Western discourses in relation to feminist struggles to help women overcome oppression at various levels.

In all of the above-mentioned exchanges, the posts were mostly contentious. The posters did not spend very much time trying to frame their responses in sentences that would seem nonconfrontational. In fact, the nature of the disagreements sometimes was such that it might not have really been possible to construct a post that would fall within what has been described as a woman's style of posting. Posters made flames and attacks toward each other, but the final result (if it can be called a "final result") appears to be that most of the participants were willing to think through their individual opinions and come to an understanding of the situation based on the need for some kind of a common ground in their efforts to work against various forms of oppression.

In the above case, we see that on the women-writing-culture list, the implicit universalizing of a certain notion of what it means to be "woman-centered" leads to exclusions and silences implicit in the limited assumptions behind what women centered means within these spaces. Thus many others were not included in the very defining of the notion of women-centered—the result was not the creation of a democratic enabling environment. In the case of the Third-World women list, while there was some continued and intense dialogue that allowed multiple views to coexist even in the contentiousness of the interactive environment, there was no structure set in place for the list to continue to be a space that enabled a continuation of such discussions. Thus the list vacillated between moments of contentious exchange and moments of absolute silence. How might we learn from these two cases in the designing of environments that might enable an exchange of diverse viewpoints while at the same maintaining a continued dialogue and sense of collaboration that began to happen with a select few members on the women-writing-culture list? If both environments had been shaped through guidelines and structure that somehow allowed for an environment that accommodated disidentification (Butler 1993) as well as strategic coalitions, would that have enabled a more dialogic space? I suggest that this might indeed be so. In addition, these spaces would probably have worked as collaborative and dialogic spaces if they were based in strategic coalitions working toward a concrete common goal meaningful to all members of the lists.

In light of all the complexities and contradictions associated with designing and inhabiting women-centered technological practices and women-centered e-spaces, how might we proceed with the task of producing ICT-related environments that are empowering and enabling for much of the underprivileged population of the world?

In this chapter, I have touched upon and described some issues that arise in specific technological environments in relation to gender and ICTs. My intention is to lay these out as issues and questions that we must engage in depth if we are to find real solutions to the problems of gender and other forms of inequity in relation to ICTs within our increasingly global world. We cannot limit our questions to mere access to technologies and technological environments as currently designed and structured, but we must delve into multiple mediated and specific contexts in order to gain an understanding of how we might be able to redesign technological environments for the empowerment of the less privileged of the world.

Such points of entry into the examination of gender in relation to ICTs as I have chosen in this chapter could lead to further investigations into how gender is produced within different technological environments ("old" and "new"). For instance, what gendered practices and tasks within these environments are associated with what kinds of power or lack of power? When does the "feminization" of particular kinds of labor get perceived as a social and economic handicap? Within what larger everyday sociocultural and political/economic hierarchies do processes of "masculinization" and "feminization" get equated with power, domination, low prestige, or with oppression?

In this chapter, I have laid out some situations in which there is no doubt that some pro-women change in the design of technological environments is necessary. We can see that in redesigning technological environments to make them women-centered, we need to be aware of the possible exclusions and inclusions implicit in the defining of such spaces.

Therefore I reiterate and extend the questions raised at the beginning of this chapter: What would women-centered practices of ICT design and use look like? How would women-friendly technological environments be structured? It is possible to see through the engagement with a variety of contexts such as those discussed in this chapter that women-centered may not necessarily mean the same thing to all women across contexts based on age, class, race, geography, and so on. How might it be possible to develop cyberfeminist strategies for the development of technological environments and practices that will be empowering for various marginalized populations of the world? Are available conceptual grids and categories for defining and conceptualizing marginalized populations and their needs useful for such a project? What does this mean, for instance, for that very universalized concept "Woman"? As we speak of gendering, we are not just talking of the biological equation: female sex equals woman. We are talking of sociocultural and material everyday communal practices and the hierarchies within which our "womanness" and "manhood" is shaped. So, as we see the multiple-mediated and various ways in which gender emerges, can we necessarily assume that women-centered means the same things within diverse community structures shaped through intersecting contexts and histories of race, class, caste, sexuality, geography, and so on? In cases such as the ones described in the discussion of women-centered e-mail lists, for instance, there seems to be an implicit assumption that women-centeredness is of necessity egalitarian or dialogic. When we speak of women-centered environments, therefore, there is an implicit assumption that they will be wonderful conflictless spaces. Yet are not the unsaid conditions for the erasure of conflict and the creation of "consensus" equal to the erasure of dissenting voices and the performances of a lack of hierarchy based on the silences of many others? How do we work with these contradictions as we try to build a dialogic technologic environment online or offline? Therefore, should we assume that designing women-centered technological environments under the currently circulating definitions of what women centered seems to imply is empowering to all marginalized women of the world?

The unquestioning celebration of women-centeredness and the discourses regarding the construction of woman as subject rely too much on a "single-theme analysis" where the category woman can be separated from other intersecting categories of lived experience such as race, class, caste, and geographical location. It is presumed that each of these categories is autonomous. Yet as Norma Alarcon points out, such analyses ignore the fact that "one 'becomes a woman' in ways that are more complex than in simple opposition to men. In cultures in which 'asymmetric race and class relations are a central organizing principle of society,' one may also 'become a woman' in opposition to other women" (1990: 361).

Therefore most models for the examination of empowerment via digital technologies are currently structured in such a way that the very framing of questions disallows the possibility of understanding Others' silence as a resistant refusal to make themselves visible within structures of power and sociocultural environments not of their own making. There is thus a need to critically examine existing theoretical models for the design of egalitarian women-friendly and diversity-sensitive technological environments so as to develop new ones that are more appropriate for our increasingly complex and interdependent global world.

Notes

1. The Spoon Collective is a group of "netizens" hosting several discussion lists. It is operated through the Institute for Advanced Technology in the Humanities at the University of Virginia. Our website is at http://lists.village.virginia .edu/~spoons.

2. See http://www.cyberdiva.org/erniestuff/rpr.html for archives.

3. I have enjoyed the exchanges on each of these lists as participant and as lurker with respect to various topics. The analyses and claims made in this chapter are not meant as personal attacks against any of the list members or as an expression of my personal preference for one list over and above the others. Neither do I necessarily endorse any of the opinions and statements made on these lists.

4. Once again, I am not suggesting here that any individual member intentionally set up such a power structure. Just as I, with my "style" of moderating, perpetuated a certain atmosphere on the list, the active participants in their well-meaning supportive style of dialogue unintentionally silenced women who were outside of the contexts represented by the participants' posts.

5. It is interesting also to note that at least one of the participants in these clusters of exchanges on Third-World women was also an active member of women-writing-culture.

Part Three

CYBERFEMINISM AND THE "THIRD-WORLD" DIALOGUES

CYBERFEMINISM, TECHNOLOGY, AND INTERNATIONAL "DEVELOPMENT"

Radhika Gajjala and Annapurna Mamidipudi

The simplest way to describe the term "cyberfeminism" might be that it refers to women using Internet technology for something other than shopping via the Internet or browsing the World Wide Web. Another way of saying the same thing is that cyberfeminism is feminism in relation to "cyberspace." Cyberspace is "informational data space made available by electrical circuits and computer networks" (Vitanza 1999: 5). In other words, cyberspace refers to the "spaces," or opportunities, for social interaction provided via computers, modems, satellites, and telephone lines—what we have come to call the "Internet." Even though there are several approaches to cyberfeminism, what cyberfeminists share is the belief that women should take control of and appropriate the use of Internet technologies in an attempt to empower themselves.

The idea that the Internet can be empowering to individuals and communities who are underprivileged is based on the notion of scientific and technological progress alleviating human suffering, offering the chance of a better material and emotional way of life. In this chapter, we make conceptual links between "old" and "new" technologies within contexts of globalization, Third-World development, and the empowerment of women. We wish to question the idea of "progress" and "development" as the inevitable result of science and technology and critique the top-down approach to technology transfer from the

Northern to the Southern hemisphere. Two questions of central importance to us are:

- Will women in the South be able (allowed) to use new technologies under conditions that are contextually empowering to them, because they are defined by women themselves?

- Within what Internet-based contexts can women from the South truly be heard? How can they define the conditions under which they can interact online, to enable them to form collaborations and coalitions aiming to transform social, cultural, and political structures?

The Internet and "Development"

Cyberfeminists urge women all over the world to learn how to use computers, to get "connected," and to use the Internet as a tool for feminist causes and individual empowerment. However, ensuring that women are empowered by the new technology requires that we investigate issues that are much more complex than merely providing material access to the latest technologies. The Internet has fascinated many activists and scholars all over the world, because of its potential to connect people from all over the world in a way that has never been possible before. It can enable individuals to publish written material instantaneously and to broadcast information to obscure locations of the world. Observers predict that the Internet will cause unprecedented and radical change in the way human beings conduct business and social activities. In much of the Northern hemisphere, as well as in some materially privileged sections of populations located in the Southern hemisphere, the Internet is celebrated as a tool for enhancing worldwide democracy. The Internet and its associated technologies are touted as great equalizers, which will help bridge gaps between social groups: the "haves" and the "have-nots," and men and women.

Since the Second World War, "development"—transferring and "diffusing" Northern forms of industrialization, scientific and technological "progress," knowledge, and modes of production and consumption from the North into Southern contexts—has been seen by many as the one over-arching solution to poverty and inequality around the world. Much current development literature, as well as media representations of the so-called underdeveloped world, reinforces this discourse of development and underdevelopment. As scholars such as Edward Said (1978) have pointed out, this process is also apparent in the context of colonialism, when the production of knowledge about the colonized nations served the colonizers in justifying their project.

What, then, does it mean to say that the Internet and technology are feminist issues for women in developing nations when the project of development in itself is saddled with colonial baggage? In order to examine if women in these contexts are indeed going to realize empowerment through the use of technology, we need to understand the complexity of the issues they face, by considering the ways in which the conditions of their lives are determined by unequal power relations at local and global levels.

The Form of This Chapter

In the next sections, we each describe our engagement with cyberfeminisms, development, and new technology and discuss some problems we encounter in our efforts. Both of us have interacted quite extensively using the Internet, where our interactions occasionally overlap when we engage in discussions and creative exchanges.[1] One of us (Annapurna Mamidipudi) is also involved with an NGO (nongovernmental organization) working with traditional handloom weavers in south India. The other (Radhika Gajjala) works within academia and creates and runs online "discussion lists"[2] and websites from her North American geographical location, aiming to create spaces that enable dialogue and collaboration among women with access to the Internet all over the world. The writing of this chapter took place over the Internet, across a fairly vast geographical distance of approximately 10,000 miles. We have written the chapter as a dialogue, to make our individual voices and locations apparent. This unconventional form and method for this chapter is appropriate for our subject matter: a belief in the possibilities of dialogue and collaboration across geographical boundaries offered by this medium of the future. We do not consider either of us to represent the North or the South, "theory" or "practice"; each of us uses our professional and personal experience of technology within both First-World and Third-World contexts. Both of us share caste, class, national, and religious affiliations, but once again, neither of us is representative of Indian women.

Annapurna Mamidipudi

As a fieldworker in an organization that focuses on the development and use of ecofriendly dyes, I am part of a team that has been successfully introducing and transferring the technology of nonchemical ecofriendly natural dyes to clients. The course we offer is comprehensive; it includes training in botany and dye material cultivation patterns, concepts of ecofriendly technology, actual dyeing techniques and tools, specific methodology for further research, aesthetics, and market research. While the service we provide is similar to that of any professional consultancy, we differ importantly in that we cater solely to traditional handloom weavers; our trainees, sponsors, and manufacturers are all artisans, men and women from traditional weaving communities.

The craft of traditional natural dyeing is based on sophisticated knowledge that has been passed down from generation to generation of artisans. The end-product created by these artisans is exquisite hand-loomed cloth, woven of yarn hand-spun from local cotton by women in remote Indian villages, dyed in the vibrant colors of indigo and madder. This has been exported all over the world from precolonial times onward. One might well ask, why should a skill that has been passed down successfully over so many generations suddenly need technical consultants like me for training?

Radhika Gajjala

I am a producer, first, of theory concerned with culture, postcolonialism, and feminism. I depend on continuous dialogue with women from nonprivileged and non-Western locations, examine the experience of activists like Annapurna, and collaborate with men and women from the South. I do rely to a large extent on having access to knowledge through technology and the power structures of the North. However, I do not believe that this need blinds me to the fact that these power structures oppress women and men living in poverty in both the North and the South. My second role as a producer is in the creation of electronic spaces for self-expression and dialogue[3] between people of different identities. The Spoon Collective,[4] started in 1994, is "dedicated to promoting discussion of philosophical and political issues" (http://lists.village.virginia.edu/~spoons). I entered the Spoon Collective in summer 1995, when I volunteered to comoderate two "discussion lists." I set up two discussion lists in 1995 and 1996, which I will discuss later in this chapter.

While members of the Spoon Collective have different individual aims in belonging to the Collective, I believe that all of us are interested in the possibilities of activism through electronic communications. All of us have set up and continue to moderate discussion lists that implicitly question the global status quo in one way or another. One member of the Collective said, "One way in which we conceptualize what we do is by talking about thinking [and writing/speaking online] as a civic, public activity." As is characteristic of much Internet-based activity (whether activist, personal, or commercial), the goals, evaluation of product/output, and apparent effects/impact on society and culture are constantly debated and in a state of flux. Key questions for us include how we can say if a list "works" or not. By the volume of messages exchanged? Or the "quality" of information and/or discussion? How would "quality" be determined? Do we rather determine the success of the list by the number of members subscribed to it? Or by the number of members who participate by sending messages? By the number of websites that have links to our list archives and/or Spoon Collective website? How could we tell from this how many people we really reach?

Starting up discussion lists, and constructing websites, meant that I had to teach myself sufficient programming and computer-related skills to be able to manage the technical side. My background as creative writer and student in the humanities had not trained me for the technical aspects of being an active producer online, and my knowledge is mostly self-taught. Later in this chapter, I discuss my e-mail lists as part of an effort to facilitate collaborations between feminists across vast geographical boundaries. What scope is there for them to discuss and assert their differences on an equal basis, within these electronic social spaces that are based in unequal economic, social, and cultural relations? In a sense I suppose my online ventures could be called "cyberfeminist" investigations.

Annapurna Mamidipudi

Up to the nineteenth century, most of the weaving industry in the area where I work was shaped to the demands of local consumers. Chinnur is a little village in Adilabad, in an interior region of the Deccan plateau in south India. There used to be a large concentration of weavers in this area, with a reputation for excellence in textiles. The reputation was based on three things: the skill of the farmers in producing different varieties of cotton, the ability of different groups of people to work together and process the cotton, and finally, the wealth of knowledge of dyes and techniques that added aesthetic value to utility. The different castes and communities were interlinked in occupational as well as social relationships, exchanging services and materials, creating a strong local market economy that was entrenched in the traditions and rituals of daily life. Traditionally, women of leisure from nonweaving communities spun, exchanging spun yarn for sarees—during specific seasons or events.

However, the development of chemical dyes almost a hundred years ago in Europe had a calamitous effect on traditional Indian dyeing practices. Processes that were the pride of the textile industry of this country were abandoned and replaced by the chemical ones. Even in remote Chinnur, the spreading wave of modern science changed people's perceptions of traditional technology; they now saw it as outmoded, and this resulted in almost total erasure of knowledge of the traditional processes within these communities.

European documentation of the local dyeing and weaving activities had been initiated in the eighteenth century; Indians themselves continued this up to the early twentieth century, in a bid to preserve knowledge. But this process meant that knowledge that had been firmly in the domain of practice of the artisans was now converted into textual information and shifted the ownership of the knowledge to those able to "study," rather than "do."

As the outside world mutated into a global village, the organic processes of the traditional artisan weaver turned a full cycle back to popularity when the color of neeli (indigo) caught the imagination of ecology-conscious consumers in the late 1970s. But even while the self-congratulatory back-patting went on among the nationalists and intellectuals, the weavers had internalized information about "modern" chemical technology. Just as they had begun to find a footing in the market, their practical knowledge was again found wanting. The only available information about vegetable dyes was in the language of the colonizers, codified and placed in libraries or museums and inaccessible to the traditional practitioners from whom the information had been gathered in the first instance. Thus, though a demand seemed to have been created for their product, in reality this further reinforced the image of weavers' technology as needful of input from outside experts, in the weavers' own minds as well as in those of others.

Today, in most descriptions of the handloom industry, the traditional weaver is seen as an object of charity, who can survive only through governmental handouts or elitist patronage. Yet their "sunset" industry (as it was referred to by a top official in the Department of Handloom and Textiles, the governmental organization in charge of formulating strategy on behalf of this industry) has the second largest number of practitioners, farming being the first, in India. For the men and women engaged in weaving in villages across India, the journey from traditional neeli to modern naphthol (chemical) dyes has meant a journey from self-sufficiency to dependence, self-respect to subordination; in short, a journey to "primitivity."

Radhika Gajjala

Most highly educated women from the Third World, even if we live in the North, experience a parallel journey to primitivity in the sense Annapurna uses earlier. In part, this happens through acquiring Western-style education and professional status. This is not often an autonomous personal choice. No woman of the Third World has the luxury of not choosing to be westernized if she aspires to be heard, or even simply to achieve a level of material freedom, comfort, and luxury within global structures of power. Many of us have "made it" within westernized professional systems and have enjoyed the status of the representative Third-World woman within global structures of power. Our education and professional status means that, although we are of the Third World, we are not representative, and our stories are not those of many truly underprivileged women in Third-World locations. Often, we take on the roles of victims of Third-World cultures or victors who have "survived" our backgrounds.

Yet when we refuse the victim/victor positions allotted to us, we sometimes get responses from Western feminists (not all—just some) that suggest that our experiences don't count since we are not the real Third-World women. I would suggest that this is another move to silence women of the Third World. Even as we demonstrate our potential and rise to the level of education and westernization required to become powerful within global structures, we are silenced and, once again, told that we don't count.

Annapurna Mamidipudi

Outside the house of one of the weavers in the village of Chinnur is a chalk written address board in English. It says: "Venkatesh U.S., Weavers' Colony, Chinnur." The initials U.S. after this man's name stand for "Unskilled Labour": a powerful statement on how an expert weaver chooses to categorize himself. This classification in the government records, he hopes, will make him eligible for a low-grade job in a government office.

I first came here as part of a team of fieldworkers of an NGO that was offering marketing support to craft groups. Natural dyeing seemed an option that could add value to the cotton cloth that was being woven. This strategy would also eventually decrease weavers' dependence on a fickle market and centralized raw material supply systems. We ourselves did not know the technology, but we were optimistic about the chances of its revival, provided there was active participation on the part of producer groups.

Transferring the technology of natural dyeing to the field presented many challenges. The sources of information that were available were texts noting original processes of artisan practice, in textual form, some documented 300 years ago. Some scholars had researched fragments of the old processes, and some practitioners recalled parts of them. We needed historians to access information from libraries where the documentation was kept; we then needed dyeing experts to interpret the recipes, botanists to participate in the process of identifying materials, engineers to create appropriate technology to ensure fastness and brightness in colors, and chemical technologists to interpret the techniques and demystify processes that had been interlinked with ways of life that were sometimes hundreds of years old. Making scientists of the weavers, we had to aid them in reinterpreting information to suit their changed environment and resources, rather than impose on them processes that would place demands on them that would be more oppressive than toxic chemical dyes—in the name of traditional technology. The innate capability and skill of the weavers made this impossible task feasible, and success came five years later, when we produced a range of colors and dyeing techniques that withstood the most stringent of quality tests. A group of dyer-weavers now acted as resource people in workshops held by us to train other groups.

Our clients today are confident weavers who come back to us time and again, to participate in the effort to empower more and more artisan groups by sharing information on a technology that has emerged from their efforts on the field.

In Chinnur lives Venkatavva, one of a group of six weavers who decided that they would take the risk of inviting an outside agency to help them become self-sufficient. When we first visited Chinnur eight years earlier, Venkatavva offered us no hospitality in her home. Her three-year-old daughter's staple drink was black coffee, drunk without milk. There was no food to be offered to visitors who turned up once the morning meal was past. Today, she entertains buyers from Europe, while listening to her husband tell the story of his successes. Her eyes are bright with laughter when she remembers less-successful experiments that resulted in pale and fugitive colors and irate customers. She points proudly to the shirt that her husband, Odellu, wears today, which he himself has woven. The journey from chemical technology to the indigo vat, from dearth to bounty, from apathy to laughter—this is her journey. In this context, which technology is traditional and which modern? Who is to decide which one is the road to empowerment and self-respect?

Radhika Gajjala

My journey to "modernity" begins with my increasing awareness of my ignorance and consciousness of contradictions and injustices implicit in the knowledge I was acquiring. My challenge as a feminist in making this journey is to ride the fine line between "victim and victor," trying not to claim either status, while asserting that Third-World feminists need to engage with the issue of women's empowerment differently, in awareness of the complexities of their lives. My journey continues into an examination of the possibility that women, men, and children can overcome the borders between them in order to reach out to common goals of emancipation.

One of the main purposes of my Internet discussion lists is to facilitate connections between Third-World activists and scholars located outside, and within, U.S. academic institutions. The hope is that this dialogue will result in collaborative work by and for women living in underprivileged and oppressive conditions, in North and South. My lists are humble efforts that form a small section of the larger efforts being made by women all over the world. Whether they have been successful in any sense is not for me to say. There are many feminists and activists using the Internet in far more effective ways, and examples of these can be seen all over the World Wide Web (see http://www.igc.apc.org/vsister/res/index.html for some examples).

I started the Third-World women discussion list in late 1995, partly as a result of my frustration with what I then saw as a lack of political commitment and exchange within some women-centered lists of which I was a member. At that time, access to the Internet was dominated by men and women from the North. (This is the situation even now, although there are more men and women from the South accessing the Internet.) Even in occasional instances where women and men from the South had access, they were quite class-specific and, in my opinion, too eager to be ideal native informants for Northern audiences. In this sense, the Internet became a space for them to perform to the Northern audience and receive favors for sufficiently Western, or appropriately exotic, performances. My frustration was both with the way people represented themselves and the manner in which topics were discussed. Even discussion lists and websites that claimed to be critical and feminist sometimes fell into this trap (possibly, my own lists and websites do so too). What was important to me at the time I started the list and what continues to be important for me in maintaining these electronic spaces for dialogue is that a conscious effort should be made to be critical and self-reflexive.

Sa-cyborgs was started with a similar goal in mind; the focus of this list is an interactive exchange of creative writing in relation to gender, race, class, and geographical location. Both lists were formed in the recognition that acts of representation are political.

Annapurna Mamidipudi

Women who tussle with the question of how to define their class and Northern or Southern identity on the Internet are a privileged few. Questions relevant to women to whom the Internet technology is being touted as the route to empowerment might ask: "But who has the Internet empowered? How has this happened? How relevant is that process for Venkatavva?"

Venkatavva has seen the advent of roads, cars, telephones, and television in the short thirty years of her life and understands the advantages, the disadvantages, and the illusion of access that these give her. In a land of faulty cables and unpredictable electrical supply, her children drink milk on the days that the bus doesn't run, because on those days the milk in the village can't be taken to the city and isn't worth money. Modern technology holds no bogies for her; she has choices that many women in the North don't have access to. On days the electricity fails she watches the traditionally performed storytelling enacted in the village square instead of the distant Santa Barbara on television. As of today, the quality and quantity of her available choices are based as much on the failure of technology as its success. So would modern technology be working toward more quality and quantity in choice, or less?

As an activist working in developing technology for her, I can only say this: Let her have access to the Internet, since why should this be barred when other aspects of modern life are imposed—from Western consumer goods to twentieth-century diseases such as AIDS. But let it not be assumed that the Internet will empower her. Otherwise this too will go the way of all imposed technology and achieve the exact opposite of what it purports to do.

The Net will be a more colorful, exotic place for us with Venkatavva flashing her gold nose pin, but what good will it do her? The Net, as it is, has a perception of Southern women as "brown," "backward," and "ignorant." A frequent, kinder depiction of them is as victim of their cultural heritage. Is being exposed to such images going to help Southern women by encouraging them to fight, with self-respect, or will it further erode their confidence in a fast-changing environment?

What, then, is the process by which a Venkatavva is empowered by the Net?

Radhika Gajjala

She should be free to decide how the Internet and other related technologies might be used to benefit and empower her and her community. The tools and access should be provided unconditionally, not as a way of selling a so-called superior lifestyle modeled on the "civilized" and urban centers of the world. Women like Ventakavva are perfectly capable of making the decisions needed to empower themselves according to their everyday needs. Policies designed to be empowering should aid and enable, not impose and preach while fostering further inequalities and inadequacies.

From within my academic, Northern location, then, I quote (not without reservations similar to those voiced by Annapurna in her rejoinder) from a paraphrasing of a talk to the Gender and Law thematic group[5] at the World Bank. For Spivak, the writer, the question that emerges in the context of her work with women in Bangladesh and development work is: "How do we approach the bottom?" that is, "How can we learn from below?" One must not approach the work with the "supremacist's assumption" that anything that exists must be bettered. The idea is to enter into and learn the traditions from inside, see what traditions can be worked with to slowly make the situation better and accepted from the inside and to ensure that new developments are initiated from the inside. The need [is] to do "invisible mending" of the native fabric by weaving the different positive threads of existing in the fabric. (See moderatorgl@worldbank.org, April 20, 1999.)

Annapurna Mamidipudi

How do we resolve the contradictory sentiments of "the Internet is a panacea to the problems of the South," "on the contrary—it may even be bad for us," and "that doesn't mean we don't want it"? We need to study processes of empowerment and work out how it is to be done in the context of the Internet. While case studies abound for the failure of this process, development workers in particular would not regard it as fair (or politically correct) to downplay the potential of the Internet to empower many women like Venkatavva in the South and the North. We cannot say, "I won't give you the Internet, for your own good."

Radhika Gajjala

My experience of observing the development of the Internet, and using this mode of communication, is that while there are hierarchies of power embedded in the very construction and design of Internet culture, there is still a potential for using it in ways that might subvert these hierarchies and foster dialogue and action on various unexpected fronts, in unpredictable ways. However, it remains true that the NGOs who speak with and for women living in poverty throughout the world, as well as the women themselves, have to negotiate and dialogue with the powerful in the North from positions of lesser power. This situation of unequal economic and social power relations between the North and the South presents challenges for people like me who are trying to design electronic spaces of dialogue and activism.

Therefore I reiterate the questions central to our discussion in this chapter and ask readers to think deeply and honestly about the issues they raise, over and beyond the topics we have addressed in this chapter. Will women all over the world be able (allowed) to use technologies under conditions that are defined by them and therefore potentially empowering to them? Within which Internet-based contexts will women of lesser material and cultural privilege within "global" power relations be able to develop collaborative work, and coalitions, to transform social, cultural, and political structures?

These questions cannot be addressed only in relation to women of the Third World. Women from the First World need answers to these questions too. Just because the Internet has its "headquarters" in the First World, this does not mean that it is contextually empowering to all women in that context. Whether located in the Northern hemisphere or the Southern, whether rich or poor, it is certain global structures of power (through their "invisible" control of the market, Internet service providers, software design, language, and so on) that determine women's use of the Internet. If cyberfeminists want to ensure that the Internet is empowering, it is not enough to "get connected" and set up websites and maintain e-mail discussion lists. The latter tasks, while necessary, are only a miniscule part of the battle.

Notes

1. Even as we work collaboratively on writing projects such as the present one, we are exchanging nontraditional creative writing, in relation to our personal/

professional/political conflicts and dilemmas, on sa-cyborgs. For information on sa-cyborgs and Third-World women, see http://lists.village.virginia.edu.

2. Electronic networks whose participants discuss a particular topic or topics.

3. See http://personal.bgsu.edu/~radhik.

4. The Spoon Collective is operated through the Institute for Advanced Technology in the Humanities at the University of Virginia.

5. Quoted from a post to the gender law discussion list—gender-law@jazz .worldbank.org, received on April 29, 1999.

CHAPTER SEVEN
CARVING DISAPPEARING ANALOGUE/DIGITAL "SELVES"

Radhika Gajjala and Annapurna Mamidipudi

"<u>writing</u>
the self

        through an Other voice
        for the Other
        pretending the Self
        exists

my concern is not writing the body
        <u>I</u>
<u>have lost all perception of</u>
        my
        body
intellectual bulemia
and anorexia
and greed
        <u>my</u>
<u>image</u> in the mirror is someone
        i do not
        know
understand
            did i ever?

<u>wrything the cyborgian</u>

<u>body</u>
I realize how
<u>centuries of</u>
<u>transformations</u>
have made it impossible
for me
to write the self"—Gajjala 1997 (http://www.cyberdiva.org)
　　"If Being Digital is a state of being hooked to the network with
　　one's point of view flying through empty space, then it is Being
　　Material that makes that connection a reality. If cyberspace is seen
　　as an extension of the material world, the performativity of mate-
　　rial bodies in virtual spaces cannot suddenly be conceived in terms
　　of being free of markings of race, gender, and class." Jayashree
　　Odin, http://65.107.211.206/post/poldiscourse/odin/odin1.html

*My writing, traveling selves have led me into ongoing (aborted, incom-
plete, questioning) acts of building and inhabiting multimediated heterotopic
technospaces (Munt 2001). Re-designing and re-booting continually—I have
re-birthed in various forms in my four decades of life. At various stages the mir-
rors in my life have reflected me, and both allowed and hindered processes of re-
invention. —Gajjala, personal reflection, February 2003*

*What is it that will give me "identity"? A lot of it is how I am perceived by
someone else. Today I seem to have given away this power to people who have a
vested interest in seeing me as one thing or the other. . . . I am constantly in the
position of negotiating for more space. . . . Do I get more people to negotiate on
my side, do I decide that I and only I will decide my identity . . . in a "RL" [real
life] world where my identity is already threatened by my own ignorance. . . .
Will not the net just be one more place where I am "ignorant"? —Mamidipudi,
personal e-mail communication to Gajjala, 1999*

R,
Of course, you may quote me.
*Academic diction is quite different from everyday parlance. It is also spe-
cific to location, but often abstract and indirect. So, too, can everyday speak
also be abstract and indirect. However, in the act of writing, the diction—
word choice—is structured to meet context/situation expectations. You*

might also think of it as "style difference"—high style or low style, high culture or pop culture. Typically, there has been a snobbery associated with high style—colloquial language is usually punished in the academy, as is local dialect. However, what do we lose as academicians if we embrace this attitude? How do we make our work increasingly inaccessible to those we "study" or dialogue with (my preferred parlance)? Language matters. We know this. But, how we execute that language matters more. It becomes an opportune moment to question the power structures that under gird such assumptions and, hence, practices. —Denise Menchaca, personal communication, March 2003

Radhika's Note: This chapter is written in an attempt to negotiate academic audiences located in a westernized academy. This chapter began as an attempt, by me, to place the continuing dialogues between Annapurna and me within "disciplinary"[1] venues for publication, as defined by my departmental Promotion and Tenure documents at the time of preparing to go up for tenure. However, now it is being rewritten also from a different stage in my subjectivity and professional history. Placing this exchange in a "disciplinary" context is no longer a material necessity for me, the one responsible for (guilty of) initiating the translation of our exchanges into Western Academic venues (however, I am still professionally situated within the U.S. Academy and the politics of production implicated in inhabiting such a location so I am not suggesting for a moment that I have somehow been completely "liberated" from what all that entails). Therefore the articulation and form are freed up in different ways—but still restricted. For we are still faced with the unequal relations of power within which this articulation will be circulated, read, and interpreted. However, now instead of trying to make the disciplinary argument, we want to try and present this as a problem for feminist and other critical methodologies. On discussing the problems encountered in the forming of this chapter with several feminist colleagues, the authors of this chapter have decided to perform this chapter in diverse forms—for this is how the collaboration between the two authors began and continues—in diverse forms of writing, speech, diction, and traveling awkwardly through spaces where our speech, diction, and writing is molded, disciplined, and changed. The stuttering and awkwardness therefore are moments of disarticulation meant as a gesture toward the impossibility of our task.

> *Owning up to a brief doesn't automatically make one accountable . . .*
>
> *Isn't that the problem . . .*
> *I guess that's why this dialogue space is so important . . .*
> *[or should I call it squabble space . . . ☺]*
> *—A on the Third-World women list, April 1998*
> *There is a traveling of theory and a hierarchy that privileges "Western" epistemologies even in "Other" spaces—especially in bourgeois and elite spaces that end up speaking in place of "the subaltern" —R, personal e-mail to A*

.

In this chapter, we try to make sense of this process for ourselves and others knowing that there are others trying to work through similar issues—adopting various tactics and strategies for the disruption of colonizing discourses and methodologies. In a continuing effort to provide the context for our discussions and to connect our continuing dialogues regarding gender, development, cyberfeminism, technology, and handloom weavers to various conversations currently happening in the Academy (whether in communication studies, cultural studies, feminist studies, development studies, cultural anthropology, or postcolonial studies), we trace the history of our collaborative writing. We invite others to dialogue with us—we can be reached via http://www.cyberdiva.org.

In what follows, the metaphors are based in multiple media—when we write "Take One" and so on, for instance—we invoke video/film production and viewing. In places we invoke theater and theatrical writing. Through the insertion of "hyperlink" here and there and "moo-logs" and "msn chat" logs, we insert three different kinds of Internet-based diction—a) MOOs (Multi-User Domains Object-Oriented) are text-based environments with programmable "objects" that form the background and serve as props within that space of performance and MOOs are still mostly accessed through "telnet"; b) MSN chat and Yahoo chat are also text-based and synchronous; c) while hyperlinks are based in Web culture. Take One takes us through the route of "communication studies" (the discipline within which one of the coauthors is located) [illegitimately] mapping in questions of feminist epistemology. Performatively, we attempt to demonstrate the struggle of being heard as non-Western (feminist?) researchers/practitioners, where in our class/caste location (whether geographically situated in the Third World as Annapurna is or geographically situated in the "west" as Radhika is) we

> must think and function within the context of a powerful tradition that, although it systematically oppresses women, also contains within itself a discourse that confers a high value on women's place in the general scheme of things. (Narayan 1990: 259)

We are thus, as Indian women of class/caste privilege, faced by the "dark side of epistemic privilege" (Narayan 1990: 265), where we must be wary of discourses that require us to take on subject positions of either "victim" or "victors" of our cultures.

Take One: "Communication Studies" as Audience

The purpose of this section is to attempt to situate our ongoing dialogues in relation to gender and technology, cyberfeminism and e-commerce, old and new modes of production within the discipline of communication and media studies. We have juxtaposed different and apparently contradictory contexts as we have textually performed subject positions resulting from our engagement with our contexts. Our print and online collaborations, therefore, form a part of our continuing attempt to interrogate binaries such as "local/global," "traditional/modern," and "theory/practice" produced within modernist framings of technology, culture, and development.

This section lays out the theoretical grounding for the project from a communication studies location. Our perspective is critical. Critical research, Sholle suggests, must "uncover the historical specificity of our dominant practices, to map out interconnections, and to discover the forms of discourse that coheres in them" (1988: 38). In an effort to engage in such a process of uncovering, we attempt these dialogues so as to open up analytical categories and social spaces (both online and offline) that do not merely pose differences and binaries, but help aid in the articulation of processes for the relational, interconnected, empowering, and contextual use of technologies.

Technologies and their uses must be examined contextually if we are to understand how they aid or inhibit specific communities' democratization and material progress. As Jennifer Daryl Slack argues:

> technology is not simply an object connected in various ways to the institutional and organizational structures from within which it emerges to be reconnected in a new context, but . . . it is *always an articulated moment of interconnections among the range of social practices, discursive statements, ideological positions, social forces, and social groups within which the object moves.* (Slack 1989: 339; italics mine)

Our engagement leads us to examine two different modes of production—one related to the production of handloom fabrics and vegetable dying in India and the other related to the production of digital spaces and academic analyses of cyberspace in the United States. Both are attempted against the grain of the "continuist, progressivist myth of Man" (Bhabha 1994: 236). Further, as Lawrence Grossberg argues, "the technologies of power of the modern—temporalizes space and rearticulates the other into the different. . . . [Therefore], by temporalizing reality and human existence, 'the modern' effectively erases space" (Grossberg 1993:1). Our long-term project therefore is one of recovery of place and context—spaces that have been submerged in the emphases on speed, motion, and linear progressive Eurocentric histories. Our questioning is initiated through theoretical frames at the intersection of communication studies, cultural studies, postcolonial feminist theory, and subaltern studies (Guha and Spivak 1988).

Thus far, observations resulting from our collaborations can be listed as themes that emerge regarding modernity, globalization, and communities of production. Most salient of these as we see them today are: action (and governance) at a distance (Sassen 1998); mobility/immobility of labor and capital (Ong 1999); and differing spaciotemporalities of communities of production and the disciplining of well-tempered transnational labor forces for a "new" digital economy (Miller 1993). Each of the themes produce, and are produced through, varying degrees of privilege and lack. Implicit in these themes is the fostering of a sense of a "new economy" that regulates everyday life by way of intellectual technologies, practical activity, and expert authority in all realms of social life (Burchell, Gordon, and

Miller 1991). It is the contradictions that are encountered as well as the power structures and material needs that necessitate relations and conversations between very diverse communities that are of interest to us.

You now hear an echo, a reiteration, as we make a connection to feminist philosophers questioning epistemologies:

> *In our engagement with each other's contexts several issues surface both implicitly and explicitly. These are themes regarding globalization, Modernity and communities of production. Most salient of these as we see them today are—action (and governance) at a distance, differing spaciotemporalities of communities of production and the disciplining of transnational labor forces for a "new" digital economy. Implicit in these themes is the production and a fostering of a sense of a "new economy" that regulates everyday life through the use of intellectual technologies, practical activity and expert authority in all areas of social life, where epistemologies based in knowledge of contextual skills and expertise through the process of learning "how to" are devalued in favor of knowledge-making processes that privilege propositional knowledge. For example, Dalmiya and Alcoff (1993) describe an epistemological hierarchy between propositional and practical forms of knowledge which is implicit in modern epistemology. In describing how all knowledge in modern epistemology become propositional (i.e., information transmitted through impersonal propositions), they cite the example of how the expertise of midwives was invalidated epistemically, while their knowledge forms were constructed as ignorant "old wives's tales."*
>
>> *The epistemic invalidation of old wives's tales has been caused in part, by the fact that modern epistemology has forgotten the lesson from Aristotle that knowledge can come in two forms: propositional and practical (Dalmiya and Alcoff 1993: 220).*
>
> —*from Gajjala and Mamidipudi 2002*

The echo fades slightly merging into the following observation by Annapurna based on her fieldwork:

> *However, the synthesis of chemical dyes almost hundred years ago in Europe has had a calamitous effect on traditional Indian dyeing practices. Except in very small isolated pockets, natural dyeing practices, which were the pride of the textile industry of this country, have been totally replaced by the chemical ones. The further effect of the spreading*

wave of modern science has been the creation of the perception of traditional technology as outmoded, resulting in almost total erasure of knowledge of the traditional dyeing processes within these communities. But the European documentation of these local practices had been initiated only in the eighteenth century. This process was further continued indigenously in the early twentieth century in a bid to preserve information about practices that seemed to be going into extinction. But this pattern meant that knowledge which had been firmly in the domain of practice of the artisans now was converted into textual information; shifting the ownership of the knowledge squarely into the lap of those able to "study" rather than "do."

The organic processes of the traditional artisan weaver turned a full cycle back to popularity when the color of neeli (indigo) caught the imagination of the ecology conscious green world in the late 1970s. But even as there was a tremendous amount of self congratulatory back patting among the nationalistic intellectual elite who felt that they were finally getting their due—for the weaver, who had internalized to a great extent "modern" chemical technology, however, it was the sound of the death knell. Just as they were beginning to find a footing in the modern market, their practical knowledge (now naphthol dyes) was again found wanting. The only available information about vegetable dyes was in the language of the colonizers, codified and placed in libraries or museums—now totally inaccessible to the traditional practitioners from whom the information had been gathered in the first instance. Thus though a demand seemed to have been created for their product, in reality it further reinforced the image of the weaver's technology as needing of modernizing input from outside experts, both in their own minds as well as in others. —Annapurna, in Gajjala and Mamidipudi 1999.

We engage in examining each other's contexts through exchanges of narratives (and every now and then, actual embodied travel to each other's "field"), in a sense performing dual ethnographies—interactively through e-mail, telephone, and face-to-face dialogues. This requires us not only to analyze each other's narratives and to do fieldwork in each others' contexts, but also to examine our own processes of engagement with the material. There is a heightened awareness of our own personal locations and complicities and resistances as Third-World women from two very different professional and geographical locations, yet who share very similar family, class, caste, national, and regional histories. Our self-reflective examinations of location, rather than being focused on "the personal as political" (as in first-wave feminist consciousness raising projects), is less "in terms of identities, but rather in terms of institutional and relational structures" (Grossberg 1997: 7) routed through our personal/professional engagement within these contexts.

Our purpose here is to begin an interrogation of the process of collaborative, cross-contextual processes that resulted in the above-stated observations. Therefore, while the two of us may address the above-mentioned themes in the dialogue that follows later, it is not within the scope of this chapter to detail these themes exhaustively.

Among others, some of the questions that are raised through our ongoing work together are:

What might cyberfeminist e-commerce from below look like? Is such a contradictory "e-commerce" at all possible? What are the collaborations, connections, and issues that might emerge? Recognizing that the "local" is very much tied in with the "global" and vice versa in present day economic practices, how do we negotiate complicity and resistance, silence and speech within various communities of production and practice in an increasingly digital economy? How can we form discursive and action-based networks between the local and the global, "place-based practices" and virtual practices? In addition, while the digital economy and associated communities of practice and production situated within the so-called global practices and configurations of power feminize certain types of labor, what is the relationship between the building of online networks for communication and communities of production within everyday contexts?

But what does the communication studies discipline[2] have to do with all this?
The issues discussed in this chapter draw from work that articulates connections between knowledge/discourse practices surrounding modes of production. These modes of production shape and are shaped by cultural practices, which in turn shape and are shaped by political, social, and

communicative hierarchies, patterns, interactions, and contexts. While it is more than obvious that these are *communication issues*, it is the attempt to discipline articulations such as these within a *"communication studies"* framework that leads us on an intellectual/practical journey of critical and self-reflexive investigation, some of which will be engaged with in the present essay. While gender and technology (see for example Rakow 1988; Stone 1991; Condit 1994; Stabile 1995; Balsamo 1996; Reed 2000) and issues related to the Internet and cyberspace (see for example Warnick 1999; Cassidy 2001) have been examined by communication and media scholars (those who have written about these issues in journals published by the National Communication Association and the International Communication Association, for instance), cross-contextual dialogues not framed as interviews are rare. "Engaging in dialogue," within academic conventions and regulations of writing "is difficult in more ways than one," as Karen Altman and Thomas Nakayama (1991: 116) point out. Our struggle is similar to Altman and Nakayama's and we agree with them when they write:

> In everyday life, we all realize how much we gain by listening and responding to each other as well as by arguing our case. The forms and practices of inquiry, however, are resilient, if not outright resistant to change. As critical researchers and writers, we also struggle over form and voice. (Altman and Nakayama 1991: 123)

The purpose of this chapter, therefore, is to raise questions, to interrogate some related theoretical concepts and issues that emerge, and then to raise further issues. Along with several other communication scholars, it is our belief that contextual critical engagement highlights issues in ways that might make academic work relevant to the everyday life and work of the communities we write about and speak for, about, or with. In our struggles with theories, practices, and contexts, we agree with Celeste Condit when she writes that "[h]onest and deep engagement with particular social struggles may provide the lever we need to recover the critical reflexiveness that has disappeared from the academy" (1994: 182) due to the use of theory in a rigidly totalizing manner.

The first section of this chapter lays out some concerns arising within our collaboration/translation across contexts, and in the second half both of us converse on issues raised. The dialogue is between "Academic"/ "Activist"; Communication Scholar/NGO Field Worker; North/South; First World/Third World. Therefore, a section of this chapter is in the form of a dialogue between the two authors and follows a precedent set by the communication scholars Altman and Nakayama (1991) in their chapter entitled "Making a Critical Difference: A Difficult Dialogue". Our performative juxtapositions in writing are an effort to displace tendencies of academic work that reproduces theories and methods that "become . . . cookie-cutter template[s] rather than . . . critically reflexive ways[s] of thinking that [would attend] . . . to specific local conditions and realities" (Condit 1994: 179).

This project draws on tools of inquiry made available through conversations in the field of critical communication research. As Daryl Slack and Martin Allor note:

> The opportunity for the field resides in the ways that critical research *redefines* old research questions and opens up new areas of inquiry. The challenge to the field resides in its confronting the role of power and epistemology in communication institutions and processes as well as in our own research. (1983: 217)

What would we label this project methodologically? As a "postcolonial feminist communication performative critical ethnography/dialogue"? Perhaps. How would we situate this project theoretically and in relation to disciplinarity? What fields of inquiry inform us as we participate in a dialogue on so-called global/transnational/international/cross-contextual issues? What qualifies this engagement as a "global" issue? What is our method of investigation? What is our "evidence"? How are our "results" valid? What models of causality are being employed? Where is this project politically and epistemologically situated (Slack and Allor 1983)? Which are the "disciplines" that enable this dialogue?

The larger project that informs the present chapter draws from arguments situated in a variety of intersecting disciplines. We frame this chapter around the assertion that power relations within communities of cultural practice/material production shape individual, classed, gendered, and multicultural subjectivities while in turn, the cultural formations and histories of (economically, socially, racially, postcolonially/colonially) dominant groups shape the implicit and explicit hierarchical structuring of communities of material practice/cultural production. In this effort, we emphasize an argument already made by several critical/cultural studies communication scholars (see the works of H. Schiller, D. Schiller, and Grossberg to name only a few): that a combination of political economy and cultural approaches to the study of communication and media is necessary.

Grossberg, arguing for more attention to political economy within cultural studies, writes that "[t]he globalization of culture makes the cost of displacing economics too high," and that we need to "rethink the relations between the economy and culture without automatically slotting the economic into the bottom line" (1997: 9). In his discussion of media-cultural imperialism as part of a broader system of imperialism, Herbert Schiller writes that:

> the media-cultural component in a developed, corporate economy supports the economic objectives of the decisive industrial-financial sectors (i.e. the creation and extension of the consumer society); the cultural and economic spheres are indivisible. Cultural, no less than automobile, production has its political economy. (1991: 13)

Such approaches are especially useful in the examination of the hegemonic discourses that dominate most scholarly and popular understandings of cyberspace, Internet, and associated digital and financial technologies. Thus, we assert that, while cultural imperialism and cultural domination are not things of the past (Schiller 1991), the examination of representations, subjectivities, and discourses that emerge within the digital (post)modern culture/economy reveals that we live amidst sociocultural discourses and material practices that divide the privileged of the world from those less privileged. These divisions occur along cultural and material formations of classed, raced, and gendered subjectivities and no longer simply along the First/Third-World geographical divide. All these factors necessitate communication and media researchers to examine complex interactions of categories such as whiteness, multiculturalism, hetero-patriarchies, postcolonial nationalisms, globalization, and transnational capital as they function within private and public, local and global spaces. Such analyses by communication and media researchers would aid a contextual understanding of the multiple negotiations within multiple contexts mediated by unequal power relations that produce (post)modern subjectivities in the present-day global economy.

In the present chapter, we consider the relevance of such projects to the communication studies discipline in general. Unavoidably, this act further disciplines[3] the conversations we have thus far engaged from within a U.S.-based field of power, in the production of a particular knowledge situated elsewhere. Thus even as we attempt to raise questions in relation to the accountability and responsibilities of the researcher in relation to the contexts s/he produces, we cannot deny our own complicity in these structures of power. These very structures of power name certain contexts as Other, Marginalized, and Local while leaving untouched and uninterrogated the "Flexible" (Ong 1999), Urban[4] Self's assumption of being the Global and universalizable perspective. The flexible (academic) Urban Self is thus complicit in the production of discourses of "universalization, embodied in the rhetoric of homogenization—they would become like us— [which] legitimated a project of world conquest and colonial violence" (Grossberg 1993:1).

Research that raises the topic of marginalization in U.S. communication studies often asks *what* is being marginalized, *who* is being marginalized (who has little or no voice), and even *how* the marginalization takes place. These questions are engaged with through the various institutional structurings of the U.S. Academy, including the emphasis on disciplinarity and its links with funding and patronage of certain types of research. Therefore, we are still compelled to ask questions about these issues from frameworks of thought and articulation authorized through hegemonic processes of investigation. It is true that some communication scholars have in fact engaged issues of process, form, gatekeeping, and access, showing how knowledge production disciplines and shapes our scholarship in various ways (for instance, see Altman and Nakayama 1991; Blair, Brown, and Baxter 1994; Conquergood 1991; Grossberg 1993; Hegde 1998; Lee 1993; McLaughlin 1995; Shome 1996; Stabile 1995; Wander 1993). However, there is little research that attempts to engage "other" contexts on their own terms. For instance, communication scholarship less often examines *how* these topics are addressed, transformed, and complicated, while the assumed transparency of the for(u)ms in which we as communication scholars capture and recover "Other" voices and contexts as we implicitly and explicitly ventriloquize frame and represent is left unexamined. There is a need for such an engagement, however, if our research is to be genuinely useful beyond the walls of academia. As Nakayama points out:

> If our research is to be useful and engaged in ongoing struggles outside the field, then it must be sensitive to the readings given by "others." [This] move does not eradicate a focus on communication (in its differing definitions), but pushes us to move toward relevance outside the field. (Nakayama 1995: 171)

Communication and cultural studies scholars such as Grossberg call for a radical contextualization of scholarship in terms of "its theory, its politics, its questions, its object, its method and its commitments" (1997: 1). Where is this radical contextualizing being done within communication studies, when and how? (For some discussions of contextualization see Stabile 1995; Grossberg 1997; Stone 1991; Slack 1989.) We can confidently reply to this question by saying *on the margins of the discipline.*

The purpose here, however, is not to get into an exhaustive critique of communication research that does or does not address marginalized populations of the world, nor is it to critique the kind of self-reflexive and radically contextualizing work that communication scholars have attempted to date. It is to ask: What might a radical contextualization mean to the work that we—the two authors of the present essay—are attempting? How should we ensure that our attempts at radical contextualizing contribute to broader social and political dialogues in the world? At the same time, how do we generate evidence "in relation to some of the issues facing various communities rather than for the esoteric goal of 'understanding' communication" (Nakayama 1995: 173)? What does all this entail for the collaborations we continue to engage in across contexts and through a communication medium (the Internet)—a medium that all too conveniently erases complexities of context?

Therefore, as we engage in collaboration across contexts and seek to situate this work within communication studies we must continue to ask simultaneously "what are the standards of admissibility in other communities?" (Nakayama 1995: 173). For,

> When the research questions we ask, how we ask them, how we interpret evidence and how we present our findings are done without regard to the concerns of various communities, we risk degrading academic work and

mocking communication scholarship. . . . Communication scholarship can (and should) make a difference in the everyday lives of people. The study of communication can (and should) be relevant beyond the confines of the field, but only if we resist the attempt to discipline our evidence and, by extension, our scholarship. (Nakayama 1995: 174)

This project is one of (imperfect) translation. What happens when real-life contexts travel through texts? What happens when they are communicated and translated to audiences across contexts and when reproduction of contexts through texts is mediated by unequal power relations? Further, these exchanges are situated within a hierarchy that privileges "transmission" of (empirical) experiences, as we convert them into (theoretical) knowledge, through a back-and-forth yet uneven exchange between various epistemological structures of thought and practice.

How do each of our personal investments, complicities, and resistances influence the further reading and traveling of concepts derived through such engagements, given our lack of control over readers' interpretation of our texts? What concepts and conclusions will be drawn out of these dialogues in spaces where we have no voice or in situations where just one of us has more voice than the other? What new "buzz words" will emerge? Finally, what does "Access" mean in this situation? What is the exigency driving the researcher's attempts to access Other contexts?

Take Two—Feminist Studies as Audience

What are the frameworks available for studying issues of gender, technology, and postcoloniality? What, for instance, do feminist scholars have to say about the Internet, about information communication technologies (ICTs), about science, technology, and women in the Third World? Are these frameworks adequate—are they at all useful for our struggles in attempts to find sustainable solutions to both the issue of dialogue and voice online and the issue of providing sustainable economic solutions for weavers in communities of production that privilege a participation in the global information society?

Issues related to women and access to technologies have been studied from several angles. Scholarship that attempts to negotiate various disciplinary and contextual boundaries is produced by scholars, activists, and cyberfeminists working in development and other related fields attempting to place subaltern and indigenous populations onto the global cyberspatial map on their own terms, and raising critical questions in relation to the challenges posed by IT design and contextual sociocultural and economic-based gendering processes in technological environments. They practically, theoretically, and contextually engage a variety of issues that intersect and complicate matters when attempts are made to use information technologies against the grain and texture of the mainstream. Feminists working on issues of technology and women fall under various categories—feminist science studies, feminist Internet studies, women in development, cyberfeminists, and gender and technology. Each of these provides us with varied lenses with which to examine our sites of engagement and each of these in turn produces different solutions based in assumptions and complicities embedded in the approach.

For instance, the gender and technology approach often falls into the trap of universalizing certain Western-centric notions of "gender"—that is, there is an assumption implicit that findings about gendered experiences based on genders produced through gendering processes within certain class, race, and geographical contexts can be applied without question across class, race, geography, and world cultures. Thus, in spite of very visible protests and articulations from women of color within the United States and from transnational/postcolonial feminists arguing for the contextual, situated nature of gender formations, race, geography, and class end up being mere add-on categories. On the other hand, in the women in development approach, the term "gender" is very simplistically equated with "women" (see for instance work such as Hafkin 2002).

Both the above categories of research, while offering points of entry for us in our efforts to foreground issues related to marginalized communities of production and absent voices online, also inhibit our ability to find applied solutions to the problems we articulate. Sometimes even the articulation of the problem is inadequate to the contexts we engage with.

The body of work on feminist philosophy and science studies does offer certain theoretical critiques that allow us to engage further in-depth into the problem of voice, access, and communities of production by centering issues of epistemology and ontology of knowledge-production. As Sarah Kember argues, there is a serious need to "explore the representational, epistemological, ethical and political dimensions" of situated science and technologies (2003). Feminist critiques from this perspective show how the practice of science and technology can be steeped in a sociopolitical discourse that leads to the objectification and erasure of the Other/(Woman/Native).

Even then, sometimes, here too we face the task of having to carve out a path for what strategies and tactics must be adopted in the specific instances and contexts we engage with. The task is made difficult by the fact that much of even the feminist critiques are located within contexts so far removed, materially, ideologically, culturally, geographically, and even temporally from the context(s) we attempt to write about. In application, this approach often implicitly maps out the possibility of including the populations outside of the logic of the global information networks within digital circuits. Such exclusive frameworks succeed in highlighting the absence and discomfort of impossible subjects within a logic where westernized science and technologies reside, but do not help carve out solutions. Thus this apparent forgetfulness on the part of several feminist science and technology studies is reminiscent of movies like *Matrix Reloaded* where the skeletal and simplistic juxtaposing of the worlds of the Matrix (digital) and of Zion (the mechanistic) disappears the existence of diverse communities of production and practice—in geographical locations where the histories, economics, and politics of community and nation have thus far permitted the (albeit sometimes illegitimate) parallel existence of so-called premodern modes of production with the postmodern.

However, there exists a body of work at the intersection of postcolonial science studies, feminist science studies, postcolonial cyberfeminisms, and development studies that critiques narratives of a linear notion of Progress and Development (see for instance Harding 1998; Escobar 1999). It is here that we find possible ways to enter academic dialogues.

Annapurna writes:

> *When people have access to the outside, there seems to be a slackness in their grounding to the local. So a lot of people doing very engaging things are doing them now physically here, but virtually outside—which means that the effort may not have roots or forum or accountability here.*
>
> *I don't know that I can theorize on this, but I will try. In terms of my objection to the Internet, it is as a system that is elitist and does not finally feed into my own work place. I will myself become an object in your system if what I say does not have legitimacy beyond the novelty value of my location. Lines*

111

are being drawn down new "classes" and now one way to obtain access to western resources is through the Internet, by being visible on it. It can be used as a spring-board to fill personal-individual agendas. But what is worse is if the location itself is "objectified" in a way that takes away legitimacy. I will continue to write on the Internet as long as I am rooted in my work. As long as I am aware that I am creating a space that is legitimate and a dialogue that is "real," chose to speak for my community. This is valid as long as my community allows me to be a spokesperson or I hold accountability for my words in a real sense here, because you on the other side of a phone line have no access that I don't give you.

Thus our struggle for articulation is not framed just by a professional requirement for disciplinarity, but also by the epistemologies and ontology of knowledge-production.

[MOO-Poetic Interlude: Cyberdiva ponders on layered epistemologies and ontologies . . .
Questions of translation, looping postcoloniality relational object (ivitie)s . . .]

Date: Sun, 20 Apr 2003 22:31:07 -0400
To: sa-cyborgs@lists.village.virginia.edu
From: radhika gajjala <radhika@cyberdiva.org>
Sender: owner-sa-cyborgs@lists.village.virginia.edu
Reply-To: sa-cyborgs@lists.village.virginia.edu

I have such stories to tell . . .
how will I tell them to you?

what will I weave them into
weaving in and out
talking in code

which code will you understand
will you understand why
why i use code?

is the code I use what you can read in between?

what are you reading in the code I write today?

why are you understanding this and not that

that and not this
i will sit under my virtual tree and tell you the stories
sentencesrunningintoeachotherstoriesrunningagainsteachot
heryoursandmineaswespeakandweaveweaveandspeak and
listen . . .
and interweave. . . .

what story does my coding say to you today?

what raaga is my tune falling into?

Denise's mobile home
Denise's aura lives here . . . the stain of her thoughts . . .
left behind
with diva . . . the shadows . . . the echoes. . . . You think
you see

Our Lady of Guadalupe in a corner . . . sometimes she
possesses you . . .
sometimes Denise possesses you . . . sometime Denise
possesses her . . .
sometimes you possess Denise . . . Sometimes our lady
turns in to
Saraswathi (who is also dwelling on another moo . . . (type
ways to look for
exits))
You see watcher here.
out
The details are kinda hazy but you are no longer where
once you had
been.
Diva's_cloud
a cloud of course! type junk to go to junction. You
sometimes see
Gayathri spivak and Linda alcoff in conference here—you
sometimes
see dipti naval and dimple kapadia chatting—or even cher
dropping
by and chanting the gayathri mantram—

maybe even. . . .
You see diva's tent, stephanie's project, perhaps it's melissa's

metaphor?, Robert's Banyan tree, ekalavyudu, and Denise's mobile

home here.

enter perhaps

The details are kinda hazy but you are no longer where once you had

been.

perhaps it's melissa's metaphor?

Seems multiplicitous and freeing, and yet in a way it is inescapable . . . permission denied to get out of melissa's own world

view, no matter how open she sees her world view as . . .

no matter how

nonconcrete she thinks it is. [Type ways to find exits out of here].

You see crone's fish, saussure, derrida, bhartrhari, kalidasa, humpty-dumpty, observing the metaphor, dome's cracked mirror . . . , and

aura here.

aura | cyborgwati teleports in.

aura | cyborgwati enters the room somehow.

look

perhaps it's melissa's metaphor?

Seems multiplicitous and freeing, and yet in a way it is inescapable . . . permission denied to get out of melissa's own world

view, no matter how open she sees her world view as . . .

no matter how

non-concrete she thinks it is. [Type ways to find exits out of here].

You see crone's fish, saussure, derrida, bhartrhari, kalidasa, humpty-dumpty, observing the metaphor, dome's cracked mirror . . . , and

aura here.

ghosts_of_sages (#11345) recycled.

perhaps it's melissa's metaphor?

Seems multiplicitous and freeing, and yet in a way it is inescapable . . . permission denied to get out of melissa's

own world
view, no matter how open she sees her world view as . . .
no matter how
nonconcrete she thinks it is. [Type ways to find exits out of
here].
You see crone's fish, saussure, derrida, bhartrhari, kalidasa,
humpty-dumpty, observing the metaphor, dome's cracked
mirror . . . , and
aura here.
@create aura called ghosts_of_sages
You now have ghosts_of_sages with object number #4244
and parent aura
(#4217).

perhaps it's melissa's metaphor?
Seems multiplicitous and freeing, and yet in a way it is
inescapable . . . permission denied to get out of melissa's
own world
view, no matter how open she sees her world view as . . .
no matter how
nonconcrete she thinks it is. [Type ways to find exits out of
here].
You see crone's fish, saussure, derrida, bhartrhari, kalidasa,
humpty-dumpty, observing the metaphor, dome's cracked
mirror . . . , and
aura here.
out
The details are kinda hazy but you are no longer where
once you had
been.
aura | cyborgwati teleports out.
Diva's_cloud
a cloud of course! type junk to go to junction. You
sometimes see
Gayathri spivak and Linda alcoff in conference here—you
sometimes
see dipti naval and dimple kapadia chatting—or even cher
dropping
by and chanting the gayathri mantram—maybe even You
see diva's tent, stephanie's project, perhaps it's melissa's

metaphor?, Robert's Banyan tree, ekalavyudu, and Denise's
mobile
home here.
aura | cyborgwati seems to have left the room without
saying goodbye.

drop saraswathi
Saraswathi | Diva's_cloud
Saraswathi | a cloud of course! type junk to go to junction.
You
sometimes see Gayathri spivak and Linda alcoff in
conference here—
you sometimes see dipti naval and dimple kapadia
chatting—or even
cher dropping by and chanting the gayathri mantram—
maybe even . . .
Saraswathi | You see diva's tent, stephanie's project, perhaps
it's
melissa's metaphor?, Robert's Banyan tree, ekalavyudu, and
Denise's
mobile home here.
Saraswathi | cyborgwati is drowning in sorrows.
Dropped.
Saraswathi | cyborgwati dropped Saraswathi.
aura | Saraswathi teleports in.
Saraswathi |
Saraswathi | perhaps it's melissa's metaphor?
Saraswathi | Seems multiplicitous and freeing, and yet in a
way it
is inescapable . . . permission denied to get out of melissa's
own
world view, no matter how open she sees her world view as
. . . no
matter how non-concrete she thinks it is. [Type ways to
find exits
out of here].
Saraswathi | You see crone's fish, saussure, derrida,
bhartrhari,
kalidasa, humpty-dumpty, observing the metaphor, dome's
cracked

mirror . . . , and aura here.
Saraswathi teleports out.
aura | Saraswathi teleports in.

Diva's_cloud
a cloud of course! type junk to go to junction. You
sometimes see
Gayathri spivak and Linda alcoff in conference here —you
sometimes
see dipti naval and dimple kapadia chatting—or even cher
dropping
by and chanting the gayathri mantram—

maybe even. . . .

You see diva's tent, stephanie's project, perhaps it's melissa's
metaphor?, Robert's Banyan tree, ekalavyudu, and Denise's
mobile
home here.
enter diva's
The details are kinda hazy but you are no longer where
once you had
been.

Diva's tent
a large tent
You see sitting_down_thing, panopticon, and
mystery_object here.
drop ghosts
ghosts_of_sages | ghosts_of_sages teleports in.
ghosts_of_sages |
ghosts_of_sages | diva's tent
ghosts_of_sages | a large tent
ghosts_of_sages | You see sitting_down_thing, panopticon,
and
mystery_object here.
ghosts_of_sages | cyborgwati is drowning in sorrows.
Dropped.
ghosts_of_sages | cyborgwati dropped ghosts_of_sages.
aura | ghosts_of_sages teleports in.
Saraswathi | ghosts_of_sages teleports in.
ghosts_of_sages | ghosts_of_sages teleports in.

ghosts_of_sages |

ghosts_of_sages | perhaps it's melissa's metaphor?

ghosts_of_sages | Seems multiplicitous and freeing, and yet in a way

it is inescapable . . . permission denied to get out of melissa's own

world view, no matter how open she sees her world view as . . . no

matter how nonconcrete she thinks it is. [Type ways to find exits

out of here].

ghosts_of_sages | You see crone's fish, saussure, derrida, bhartrhari, kalidasa, humpty-dumpty, observing the metaphor, dome's

cracked mirror . . . , aura, and Saraswathi here. Ghosts_of_sages leaves for the her_metaphor.

aura | Ghosts_of_sages has arrived.

Saraswathi | Ghosts_of_sages has arrived.

—Radhika Gajjala,
http://www.cyberdiva.org[5]

Rewind: Woman as Theater? Gender and Development

Yet, unless the mainstream feminist hears responsible critique, the feminist status quo will continue to provide an alibi for exploitation.

—Spivak 1996

Time: Sometime in late 1998 R's office in XX university.
R sits facing her Mac with multiple windows active (Eudora, Netscape, Word, Telnet . . .). R can be seen pottering around the Spoon Collective server and her accumulated archival "data" in the form of lists founded and maintained by her— or maybe she was building on her MOO home at MediaMoo or LinguaMoo . . .

[MOO-Poetic Interlude: Cyborgwati invokes the goddess of learning]

fetch saraswathi
Saraswathi is already at perhaps it's melissa's metaphor?

aura | Saraswathi's eyes light up as it focuses on Saraswathi.
(chitraguptini) Saraswathi's eyes light up as it focuses on
Saraswathi.
Saraswathi | Saraswathi's eyes light up as it focuses on Saraswathi.
Saraswathi's eyes light up as it focuses on Saraswathi.
Saraswathi | Saraswathi lunges at you.
aura | Saraswathi lunges at Saraswathi but misses.
(chitraguptini) Saraswathi lunges at Saraswathi but misses.
Saraswathi | Saraswathi lunges at Saraswathi but misses.
Saraswathi lunges at Saraswathi but misses.
aura | Saraswathi looks quizzically at Saraswathi.
(chitraguptini) Saraswathi looks quizzically at Saraswathi.
Saraswathi | Saraswathi looks quizzically at Saraswathi.
Saraswathi looks quizzically at Saraswathi.
aura | Saraswathi gets confused and gives up.
(chitraguptini) Saraswathi gets confused and gives up.
Saraswathi | Saraswathi gets confused and gives up.
Saraswathi gets confused and gives up.
Saraswathi is already at perhaps it's melissa's metaphor?.
Saraswathi | You fail to retrieve saraswathi.
aura | aura's eyes light up as it focuses on aura.
(chitraguptini) aura's eyes light up as it focuses on aura.
Saraswathi | aura's eyes light up as it focuses on aura.
Aura's eyes light up as it focuses on aura.
aura | aura lunges at you.
aura | aura lunges at aura but misses.
(chitraguptini) aura lunges at aura but misses.
Saraswathi | aura lunges at aura but misses.
aura lunges at aura but misses.
aura | aura looks quizzically at aura.
(chitraguptini) aura looks quizzically at aura.
Saraswathi | aura looks quizzically at aura.
aura looks quizzically at aura.
aura | aura gets confused and gives up.
(chitraguptini) aura gets confused and gives up.
Saraswathi | aura gets confused and gives up.
aura gets confused and gives up.
aura | You fail to retrieve aura

At the back of her mind is the constant nagging fear and knowledge of her impending "third year review." Having barely surfaced from, among other things, defending and completing a fairly unusual dissertation,[6] and not knowing how she should package her work in relation to the "disciplinarity" continually being emphasized around her. . . .

Nevertheless, she composes an e-mail announcement in her continuing efforts to create dialogue (squabble?) spaces online and hits send.

"Third-World" Critique(s) of Cyberfeminism?
The purpose of this discussion will be to explore various political, social, and cultural implications and possibilities of "virtuality" in relation to technoscience, Third-World/black feminisms, and theory/practice of cyber culture as well as accountability to embodied ways of being (viewing online interactions as material/discursive practices . . .).
Discussions related to this were started on the postcolonial list, Third-World women list and in the graduate seminar on "Communication, Technoscience, and Cyberculture" (Fall 1998, Bowling Green State University)
http://ernie.bgsu.edu/~radhik/courses/courses/mcom780.html.
One of the central questions we ask is "What kind of subject/ agent is implicit in cyberfeminist narratives?"
Also problematizing the notion of a Third-World feminist critique that comes from Net and First-World spaces. . . . etc etc etc. . . .
My e-mail is radhik@bgnet.bgsu.edu
Messages to the list should be sent to seminar-13@lists.village .virginia.edu
To subscribe to seminar-13, send a message to majordomo@lists .village.virginia.edu
with the message:
subscribe seminar-13.
The subject header should be blank.
Note: Rude, sexist, racist etcetera posts will not be tolerated.
Looking forward to a great discussion!
Thank you,
Radhika Gajjala
(comoderator postcolonial,

        comoderator technology
        moderator sa-cyborgs
        moderator women-writing-culture
        moderator Third-World women)

Through ether, the message traveled—and ended up somewhere on another network—a network focused on issues relating to gender and development. R was then contacted by the editor of the Oxfam journal (still not within the "communication discipline" as defined by a U.S.-centered Academy) Gender and Development and invited to write on the potential of the Internet as an empowering tool for women in India. Recognizing that she was once again being accessed as a "native informant" based on her own visibility in online feminist spaces and identity as someone of Indian origin (in spite of the fact that it was now about nine years since she had resided full-time in India), R felt uncomfortable agreeing to writing such an article. R's research prior to 1998 focused on South Asian women in diaspora. Further, in her research, she had pointed to the fact that South Asian women in diaspora often served as easily available "native informants" for policy makers in the Western world. This invitation posed a dilemma for R. Two main issues weighed on her mind:

1. *Being close to third-year review time, she knew that at this stage a publication in a journal (even if not in a mainstream communication journal) would help her retain her job.*

2. *If she said no—that would not ensure that "the subaltern," whose voice she was worried about appropriating, would be allowed to speak in her stead. Someone else would write that article anyway. So why not use this as an opportunity to insert critique?*

"Yet, unless the mainstream feminist hears responsible critique, the feminist status quo will continue to provide an alibi for exploitation."
—Spivak 1996

        "As you note, failing to speak is a cop-out. Thus, I think the question that needs to be raised at the end of your paper is not 'From what position of authority would we speak?' BUT, rather—the position of authority we HAVE been given to speak comes from a very particular map, and at the expense of the female Subaltern who is OUR Other. If we remain silent, that is not going to make the female subaltern

HEARD. So I have always been a little bothered by the question of 'our authority to speak.' The question about 'what is OUR right to speak?' while it LOOKS like a question that places the Subaltern/Other on the map, doesn't after all produce the spaces FROM which the Subaltern COULD speak.

So I'd end by changing the Question a little. Instead of ending with: 'From what position of authority would WE speak?' I'd phrase the question more explicitly as 'Who is paying the PRICE for this authority and WHOM am I taken to speak FOR?' AND THEN, the next semantic question that follows 'logically' becomes, if you follow this—not whether we speak and what our authority to speak is, but instead—WHAT did we SAY when we were given/took up the authority to speak? And, HOW did we say it?" (C[7] in Gajjala 1998)

Having known A most of her life, and being quite sure that this might be an opportunity to juxtapose A's work context with R's in an effort at productive dialogue, R asked A to join her in the writing of this article. They wondered—would the editor agree?

As it turned out, the editor[8] not only agreed, she actually worked with both R and A in trying make their juxtaposition possible.

> *r:*
>
> *On the researcher's side, complicity in a sense is strategic and necessary —while it is about gaining access individually, it is also about creating more diverse speaking positions that will make the discipline accessible to people who continue to engage in thus far marginalized discursive and material practices. How do I negotiate this individual investment and necessity? On the activist's side what are the issues faced?*
>
> *a:*
>
> *I am of course pessimistic and nervous of our ambitions . . . but raring to go. In future work, I want a stronger context. I will be fighting you more. The other article [Gajjala and Mamidipudi 1999] has clarified for me the position I speak from. I also liked the fact that there we are talking to a group that seems to be concerned about the phenomena that is the Internet in a "real" sense.*
>
> *A genuine concern and a genuine need for solutions is something I can participate in. As a technologist who is somewhat experienced in integrating technology and people, I am clear that on any effort, commu-*

nity needs to be built to create space for discussion. I can be part of such a community. I refuse to be a lone "rebel." I therefore object to feminism as it is exclusionist in its definition, as I understand it. If it is not so, the fact that it is perceived to be so is bad enough for me. We are divided enough without defining spaces that are divided (in a real sense or in a virtual one). It is the separation of real life from the virtual one, whether on line or as a feminist that disturbs me. Your articulation of your work as a feminist excludes me; at times your articulation as a third world woman excludes me. Sometimes just the fact that you are speaking only online and not offline excludes me the most.

   r:

   I recognize that in my professional/personal negotiations and in an odd privileged way in trying to maintain my own positions to speak from within the U.S. Academy, what I have at stake in trying to put out pieces of writing such as this are slightly different than yours. I also realize that I am compelling you to perform within frameworks I have laid out, thus most definitely shaping our dialogue to conform to power structures that are probably more oppressive than empowering to the contexts within which you work. This is indeed a difficult dialogue. And quite clearly, in this dialogue there is a struggle with form and a struggle to maintain our own voices. We must believe that this is something possible at some level, or we would not be attempting it?

For the time being—the curtain falls and you no longer see the stage. Backstage, the struggles continue. The camera pans the audience—and yes, there is definitely a diversity of audience there . . .

Faith Wilding writes: "On the internet, feminism has a new transnational audience which needs to be educated in its history and its contemporary conditions as they prevail in different countries" (http://www.obn.org/cfundef/faith_def.html).

   Our rejoinder:

In the present global information society, it is important that feminisms recognize their historical complicity and their location within an ontology and epistemology that does not always understand the complexity of its audience. As feminists in a global society, it is important that we honestly examine contextual gendering processes and the hierarchies we reproduce by imposing frameworks situated in only certain contexts and thus permit ourselves to be educated in the multiple histories of how gendering processes and other (economic, social, and cultural) hierarchies have developed elsewhere. We as situated feminists, activists and academics need to be educated by our transnational audiences.

Notes

1. Personal e-mail from R to A: Here's a frame to start with—I have been immersing myself in reading material published within my "discipline"— "communication studies" because of repeated (even if well-meaning) concerns expressed by people mentoring me for tenure and promotion, that I publish within "disciplinary" journals (and in this case that means journals sponsored by the National Communication Association and the International Communication Association). My question to you is this—do you find any point of entry here that might be useful to you in your efforts to articulate the concerns from your location? I'm wondering—how do we work in your concerns and then getting past that layer, work in the weaver's concerns—how shall we articulate your discomfort with the frameworks I am quite literally luring you into? [How shall we articulate *my* discomfort? (Does it matter?)]

2. Here we invoke Lisa McLaughlin's definition of "disciplinarity," and "refer to the theories, practices, and institutional arrangements that discriminate among forms of knowledge, specify knowledge and knowledge relationships that coalesce around 'objects of study,' and demarcate boundaries within which knowledges may take on the appearance of coherence" (1995: 145).

3. Previous publications in relation to these conversations (Gajjala and Mamidipudi 1999, 2002, 2003, 2004; Gajjala 1999 and 2000) have already done so in a variety of ways.

4. Rather than using categories such as "westernized," we extend Aihwa Ong's discussion of the flexible citizen to refer to the person of privilege who is upwardly and transnationally mobile—one who has accumulated the required cultural and material capital to be able to be a "nomadic subject" and contributes to (at the same time negotiating) transnational practices and imaginings that shape hegemonic economic and cultural discourses in today's world. The term westernization does not adequately describe what we would like to describe in this chapter, for, as Grossberg suggests, it "opens a problematic which could only be resolved by the search for or construction of a self-enclosed, isolated identity" and for which reasons scholars such as Amin (1989) reject "any politics in which mod-

ernization is treated as westernization and opposed by the search for an alternative cultural identity" (Grossberg 1993:1).

5. There are different ways to perceive, to speak, to translate—the subtle nuances of the multiple layers of realities we inhabit in mind/body, thought/emotion, imagined and real spaces. This interlude performs repetition, recoding, and dwelling—through multiple metaphors—in pursuit of dialogue. MOO-Poetry Interludes in this chapter are based in cybercultural creative juxtapositions of programmed "objects" that interact with the MOO user to produce texts. I have named existing programmable objects and modified some in an attempt to produce a computer-enabled form of "poetry," in efforts to make visible the multiple negotiations we make with existing social worlds and epistemologies in an attempt to "speak." The objective nature of situated language—language as situated code/artificial intelligence the "out there-ness" of meanings associated with socioculturally named objects . . . all these are explored in my continuing MOO-poetic programming/writing online. Go to telnet://pmcmoo.org:7777. You may find me on PMC2 -moo [feel free to sign on as guest and when you get there, type @go perhaps; @go denise]. . . . Indeed, as James Elkins's book title announces, the Object *does* stare back.

6. Radhika Gajjala, The SAWnet Refusal: An Interrupted Cyberethnography, Doctoral diss., University of Pittsburgh, Dissertation Abstracts International, 99-00131, 1998.

7. "C" is one of the members the South Asian Women's network (SAWnet) who responded to one of my early dissertation drafts.

8. We will always be grateful to Caroline Sweetman for allowing that collaboration in print—for if we had not worked on a concrete print product at that time, we may not have continued to investigate these issues in collaborations, and each of us would be doing our own thing in separate public spaces even though our thought processes would always be shaped by our interaction with each other.

EPILOGUE
I WANT TO CURL UP AND DENY YOU

From rxgst6+@pitt.edu Wed Feb 19 10:08:21 1997
Date: Wed, 19 Feb 1997 10:03:14 -0500 (EST)
From: "Cyberdiva (a.k.a \"Radhika Gajjala\")"
To: sa-cyborgs@jefferson.village.virginia.edu,
women-writing-culture@jefferson.village.virginia.edu
Cc: FOP-L
Subject: i want to curl up and deny

suddenly
  (or not)
these "spaces" are
not mine

                                 they never were

not
"my" communities.
yet again
i
do not
belong.

                  I hesitate
                  i stutter
                  i trip
                  i stumble
wondering *if* i belong . . .
suddenly

EPILOGUE

        (or not)
i fear
This non-community of
"non"-people.
              mere texts?
                  (not quite)
mine and yours
that cry out in
pain and joy,
or just plain boredom . . .
as pranksters
             as though we exist.
               as if we are.
optical illusions.
translated texts.
                 we
                 are
texts are mine and yours
      claiming property rights on thoughts
      that have circulated
      and re-circulated
      for centuries
associate them with
      and sell
      to be reappropriated
      and absorbed
             but
         who are you?
I fear
      the (im)possibility
      of becoming cyborg.
      (and what kind of cyborg would that be?)
The impossibility of
not
getting absorbed
      (to recall an earlier metaphor
            on one of these "communities"
            perhaps
      borg-like
      assimilated)

If its thought of as a "frontier"
then assimilation
elimination
occupation
appropriation
must be
the goal
indeed.
even in this non-space the language is the same.
                the same.
                for shame.
as i am
as i continue to
be
        absorbed.
whether i resist or
                    not.
displaced yet again
from a community
that is not
        yet is
IRL or not
        by my own fears.
The ether takes control.
        But the eyes watch and judge.
        all those eyes that belong to fingers that
often don't type
when online.
        but
i must write.
or i cannot breath.
        My silence threatens to suffocate me.
I must reassure myself—tap at the keyboard.
(Feel the flow of ink
once again
sometimes
too.)
see the marks on empty "space."
                i don't *want* to share my thoughts.
                I want to curl up and

        deny
you.
The song that plays in the background reminds me
of a voice i had that knew.
And soared in confidence.
reminds me of tunes,
raagas
from the past
tunes i can barely name
in the flurry of the everyday
today.
Reminds me of a language i speak.
that i stumble over -
over the many dis-
placements
that my tongue has tripped over.
        A patched, sewn-together
        clumsy
        tongue. . . .
Almost forgotten tunes
Almost forgotten metaphors
        I want to curl up and
        deny
        the now
sometimes
when i don't know what (if) the
now
is.
        if in the now i
        am.
A child who does not understand
all
my past metaphors.
He watches
sometimes confused
sometimes
amused
        sometimes even seeming to
        uncover parts of his early
        childhood

memories
in other languages
he knew the metaphors once.
he knows he knew.
i know i knew.
I'm not sure which metaphors are "mine"
anymore.
Displaced several times
I'm never sure.
Some metaphors flow in this script
this script that stole my
tongue
when I was barely able to
speak.
the patched together metaphors
flow to an e-mail address
"back home."
The metaphors awaken sleeping raagas.
The writing is my singing now.
Always trying to steal back my tongue.
my "voice."
In the flurry of the everyday
the metaphors re-emerge
in sparks
in flashes
and flit by in elusive sparks of memory.
as my brain falls to pieces
trying to recollect
Was it imagined or
Was it there
ever?
Mixed up metaphors.
yes
i have read my
"spivak"
too
the "haraways"
the "fiskes"
the bhabhas

and the rest

EPILOGUE

who is located where?
is it easy to escape location
        dis-location
"here"
        on cyber"space"
perhaps
not
                and i continue to fear
        wanting just to curl up and deny.

    —Radhika, February 18, 1997

REFERENCES

Aarseth, E. J.
   Nonlinearity and Literary Theory. In G. P. Landow (Ed.), *Hyper/Text/Theory,* 51–86. Baltimore: Johns Hopkins University Press, 1994.

Ahmed, S.
   Home and Away: Narratives of Migration and Estrangement. *International Journal of Cultural Studies* 2, no. 3 (1999): 329–47.

Alarcon, N.
   The Theoretical Subjects of "This Bridge Called My Back" and Anglo-American Feminism. In G. Anzaldua (Ed.), *Making Face, Making Soul Haciendo Caras: Creative and Critical Perspectives by Women of Color,* 356–69. San Francisco, Calif.: Aunt Lute Books, 1990.

Alcoff, L.
   The Problem of Speaking for Others. *Cultural Critique* 36, no. 11 (1992): 5–32.

Alcoff, L., & Potter, E. (Eds.).
   Feminist Epistemologies. New York: Routledge, 1993.

Altman, K. E., & Nakayama, T. K.
   Making a Critical Difference: A Difficult Dialogue. *Journal of Communication* 41 (1991): 116–30.

Amin, S.
   Eurocentrism. New York: Monthly Review Press, 1989.

Anderson, B.
   Imagined Communities. London: Verso, 1991.

REFERENCES

Appadurai, A.
Disjuncture and Difference in the Global Cultural Economy. *Public Culture* 2, no. 2 (Spring 1990): 1–24.

Arun, S., & Arun, T.
ICTs, Gender and Development: Women in Software Production in Kerala. *Journal of International Development* 14, no. 1 (2002): 39–50.

Augustin, L.
They Speak, but Who Listens? In W. Harcourt (Ed.), *Women@Internet,* 149–55. London: Zed Press, 1999.

Bahri, D.
The Digital Diaspora: South Asians in the New Pax Electronica. In M. Paranjpe (Ed.), *In Diaspora: Theories, Histories, Texts,* 222–32. New Delhi: Indialog Publications, 2001.

Bahri, D., & Vasudeva, M.
Between the Lines: South Asians and Postcoloniality. Philadelphia, Pa.: Temple University Press, 1996.

Balsamo, A.
Technologies of the Gendered Body: Reading Cyborg Women. Durham, N.C.: Duke University Press, 1996.

Barber, B.
Jihad vs. McWorld. New York: Times Books, 1995.

Barthes, R.
The Pleasure of Text. R. Miller, Trans. New York: Hill & Wang, 1975.

Baym, N. K.
Tune In, Log On: Soaps, Fandom, and Online Community. Thousand Oaks, Calif.: Sage, 2000.

Behar, R., & Gordon, D. (Eds.).
Women Writing Culture. Berkeley: University of California Press, 1996.

Belsey, C.
Critical Practice. New York: Routledge, 1986.

Benedikt, M. (Ed.).
Cyberspace: First Steps. Cambridge, Mass.: MIT Press, 1991.

Beverley, J.
Against Literature. Minneapolis: University of Minnesota Press, 1993.

Bhabha, H.
The Location of Culture. London: Routledge, 1994.

Bhattacharjee, A.
The Public/Private Mirage: Mapping Homes and Undomesticating Violence Work in the South Asian Immigrant Community. In M. J. Alexander & C. T. Mohanty (Eds.), *Feminist Genealogies, Colonial Legacies, Democratic Futures*, 308–29. New York: Routledge, 1997.

Bhattacharjee, A.
The Habit of Ex-Nomination: Nation, Woman and the Indian Immigrant Bourgeois. *Public Culture* 5, no. 1 (1992): 19–44.

Biemann, U.
Performing the Border. In C. Sollfrank & Old Boys Network (Eds.), *Next Cyberfeminist International*, 36–40. Hamburg: Hein & Co, 1999.

Blair, C., Brown, J. R., & Baxter, L. A.
Disciplining the Feminine. *The Quarterly Journal of Speech* 80 (1994): 383–409.

Blair, K., & Gajjala, R.
Aligning Criteria for Online Courseware Selection with Multimodal Teaching and Learning [Electronic version]. *The Ohio Learning Network* (2002). Retrieved November 20, 2003, from http://www.oln.org.

Blair, K., & Takayoshi, P. (Eds.).
Feminist Cyberscapes: Mapping Gendered Academic Spaces. Ablex, Conn.: Greenwood, 1999.

Boese, C.
The Ballad of the Internet Nutball: Chaining Rhetorical Visions from the Margins of the Margins to the Mainstream in the Xenavers. Unpublished doctoral diss., Rensselaer Polytechnic, 1998–2000. Retrieved November 10, 2003, from http://www.nutball.com/dissertation/index.htm.

Burchell, G., Gordon, C., & Miller, P. (Eds.).
The Foucault Effect: Studies on Governmentality. Chicago: University of Chicago Press, 1991.

Butler, J.
Bodies That Matter: On the Discursive Limits of "Sex." New York: Routledge, 1993.

Cassidy, M.
Cyberspace Meets Domestic Space: Personal Computers, Women's Work, and the Gendered Territories of the Family Home. *Critical Studies in Media Communication* 18 (2001): 44–65.

REFERENCES

Chatterjee, P.

The Nationalist Resolution of the Women's Question. In K. Sangari & S. Vaid (Eds.), *Recasting Women,* 232–53. New Delhi: Kali for Women, 1989.

Chen, G. M., & Starosta, W. J.

Communication and Global Society. New York: Lang, 2000.

Christine, H.

Virtual Ethnography. London: Sage, 2000.

Clifford, J.

Routes: Travel and Translation in the Late Twentieth Century. Cambridge, Mass.: Harvard University Press, 1997.

Code, L.

Voice and Voicelessness: A Modest Proposal? In J. Kourany (Ed.), *Philosophy in a Feminist Voice: Critiques and Reconstructions,* 204–30. Princeton, N.J.: Princeton University Press, 1998.

Condit, C. M.

Hegemony in a Mass-Mediated Society: Concordance about Reproductive Technologies. *Critical Studies in Mass Communication* 11 (1994): 205–30.

Conquergood, D.

Rethinking Ethnography: Towards a Critical Cultural Politics. *Communication Monographs* 58 (1991): 179–94.

Dalmiya, V., & Alcoff, L.

Are "Old Wives' Tales" Justified? In E. Potter & L. Alcoff (Eds.), *Feminist Epistemologies,* 217–44. New York: Routledge, 1993.

Delgado, F. P.

When the Silenced Speak: The Textualization and Complications of Latina/o Identity. *Western Journal of Communication* 62, no. 4 (1998): 420–38.

Dhaliwal, A.

Can the Subaltern Vote? Radical Democracy, Discourses of Representation and Rights, and Questions of Race. In D. Trend (Ed.), *Radical Democracy,* 42–61. New York: Routledge, 1996.

Enteen, J., & Gajjala, R.

Globalization and Intercultural Communication: A Virtual Exchange Project [Electronic version]. *Kairos: A Journal for Teachers of Writing in Webbed Environments* (2002). Retrieved November 3, 2003, from http://english.ttu.edu/kairos.

Escobar, A.
Gender, Place, and Networks: A Political Ecology of Cyberculture. In W. Harcourt (Ed.), *Women on the Internet: Creating New Cultures in Cyberspace,* 31–54. London: Zed Press, 1999.

Ess, C., & Sudweeks, F.
Culture, Technology, and Communication: Towards an Intercultural Global Village. Albany: State University of New York Press, 2001.

Everard, J.
Virtual States: The Internet and the Boundaries of the Nation-State. London: Routledge, 2000.

Fernandez, M.
Digital Imperialism. *Fuse Magazine* 21, no. 4 (1999): 37–45.

Flores, L. A., & Hasian, M. A.
Returning to Aztlan and Laraza: Political Communication and the Vernacular Construction of Chicano/a Nationalism. In A. Gonzalez & D. V. Tanno (Eds.), *Politics, Communication, and Culture,* 186–203. Thousand Oaks, Calif.: Sage, 1997.

Fraser, N.
Rethinking the Public Sphere: A Contribution to the Critique of Actually Existing Democracy. *Social Text* 8, no. 9 (1990): 56–80.

Gajjala, R.
An Interrupted Postcolonial/Feminist Cyberethnography: Complicity and Resistance in the "Cyberfield." *Feminist Media Studies* 2, no. 2 (2002): 177–93.

Gajjala, R.
Studying Feminist E-Spaces: Introducing Transnational/Postcolonial Concerns. In S. Munt (Ed.), *Technospaces,* 113–26. London: Continuum International, 2001.

Gajjala, R.
Third-World Critiques of Cyberfeminism. *Development in Practice* 9, no. 5 (1999): 616–19.

Gajjala, R.
The SAWnet Refusal: An Interrupted Cyberethnography. Doctoral diss., University of Pittsburgh, 1998. *Dissertation Abstracts International* (UMI No. 9900131) (1998).

REFERENCES

Gajjala, R.
Cyberethnography (1997) [Electronic version]. Retrieved November 20, 2003, from http://www.cyberdiva.org/erniestuff/define.html.

Gajjala, R., & Mamidipudi, A.
Gendering Processes within Technological Environments: A Cyberfeminist Issue [Electronic version]. *Rhizomes* 4 (2002). Retrieved November 3, 2003, from http://www.rhizomes.net.

Gajjala, R., & Mamidipudi, A.
Cyberfeminism, Technology and International "Development." *Gender and Development* 7, no. 2 (1999): 8–16.

Grossberg, L.
Cultural Studies, Modern Logics, and Theories of Globalization. In A. McRobbie (Ed.), *Back to Reality? Social Experience and Cultural Studies.* New York: Manchester University Press, 1997.

Grossberg, L.
Cultural Studies and/in New Worlds. *Critical Studies in Mass Communication* 10 (1993): 1–22.

Guha, R., & Spivak, G. (Eds.).
Selected Subaltern Studies. New York: Oxford University Press, 1988.

Gurak, L. J.
Persuasion and Privacy in Cyberspace: The Online Protests over Lotus Market Place and the Clipper Chip. New Haven, Conn.: Yale University Press, 1997.

Hafkin, N.
Are ICTs Gender Neutral? A Gender Analysis of Six Case Studies of Multi-Donor ICT Projects. Working paper for GAINS/UN-INSTRAW (2002). Retrieved in 2002 from http://www.un-instraw.org/en/research/gender_and _ict/virtual_seminars.html.

Hall, K.
Cyberfeminism. In S. Herring (Ed.), *Computer-Mediated Communication: Linguistic, Social and Cross-cultural Perspectives,* 148–55. Amsterdam: John Benjamins, 1996.

Haraway, D.
Manifesto for Cyborgs: Science, Technology, and Socialist Feminism in the 1980s. In F. Nancy & L. J. Nicholson (Eds.), *Feminism/Postmodernism,* 190–233. New York: Routledge, 1990.

Harcourt, W. (Ed.).
Women@Internet. London: Zed Press, 1999.

Harding, S.
Is Science Multicultural? Postcolonialisms, Feminisms and Epistemologies.
Bloomington: Indiana University Press, 1998.

Hegde, R. S.
A View from Elsewhere: Locating Difference and the Politics of Representation from a Transnational Feminist Perspective. *Communication Theory* 8, no. 3 (1998): 271–97.

Heinz, B., Li, G., Inuzuka, A., & Zender, R.
Under the Rainbow Flag: Webbing Global Gay Identities. *International Journal of Sexuality and Gender Studies* 7, nos. 2–3 (2002): 107–24.

Herring, S.
Foreword. In C. Ess & F. Sudweeks (Eds.), *Culture, Technology, and Communication: Towards an Intercultural Global Village,* vii–x. Albany: State University of New York Press, 2001.

Herring, S.
Posting in a Different Voice: Gender and Ethics in CMC. In C. Ess (Ed.), *Philosophical Perspectives in Computer Mediated Communication,* 115–45. Albany: State University of New York Press, 1996.

Jacobson, D.
Doing Research in Cyberspace. *Field Methods* 11, no. 2 (1999): 127–45.

Jameson, F.
Postmodernism: Or, the Cultural Logic of Late Capitalism. Durham, N.C.: Duke University Press, 1991.

Jarratt, S.
Beside Ourselves: The Rhetoric of Postcolonial Feminism. *Journal of Advanced Composition* 18, no. 1 (1998): 57–75.

John, M.
Discrepant Dislocations: Feminism, Theory, and Postcolonial Histories. Berkeley: University of California Press, 1996.

Jones, K. B.
On Authority: Or, Why Women Are Not Entitled to Speak. In I. Diamond & L. Quinby (Eds.), *Feminism & Foucault: Reflections on Resistance,* 119–34. Boston: Northeastern University Press, 1988.

REFERENCES

Jones, S. G. (Ed.).
    CyberSociety: Computer-Mediated Communication and Community. Thousand
    Oaks, Calif.: Sage, 1995.

Karamcheti, I.
    The Shrinking Himalayas. *Diaspora* 2, no. 2 (Fall 1992): 269.

Kember, S.
    Cyberfeminism and Artificial Life. London: Routledge, 2003.

Kerfoot, D., & Knights, D.
    Management, Masculinity and Manipulation: From Paternalism to Corpo-
    rate Strategy in Financial Services in Britain. *Journal of Management Studies*
    30 (1993).

Knights, D., & McCabe, D.
    A Different World: Shifting Masculinities in the Transition to Call Centers.
    Organization 8, no. 4 (2001): 619–45.

Lal, V.
    Establishing Roots, Engendering Awareness: A Political History of Asian
    Indians in the United States. In L. Prasad (Ed.), *Live Like the Banyan Tree:
    Images of the Indian American Experience,* 42–48. Philadelphia, Pa.: Balch In-
    stitute for Ethnic Studies, 1999a.

Lal, V.
    The Politics of History on the Internet: Cyber-Diasporic Hinduism and the
    North American Hindu Diaspora. *Diaspora* 8, no. 2 (1999b): 137–72.

Landow, G.
    Hypertext: The Convergence of Contemporary Critical Theory and Technology.
    Baltimore: Johns Hopkins University Press, 1992.

Lee, W.
    Social Scientists as Ideological Critics. *Western Journal of Communication* 57
    (1993): 221–32.

Macherey, P.
    A Theory of Literary Production. G. Wall, Trans. London: Routledge, 1986.

Mallapragada, M.
    *Indian Women in the U.S. Diaspora and the "Curry Brigade": The Politics of Na-
    tion, Gender and Sexuality on the Web.* Paper presented at the Constructing
    Cyberculture(s): Performance, Pedagogy, and Politics in Online Spaces Con-
    ference, College Park, University of Maryland, 2001.

Markham, A. N.
    Life Online: Researching Real Experience in Virtual Space. Walnut Creek, Calif.: AltaMira Press, 1998.

Markley, R.
    Virtual Realities and Their Discontents. Baltimore: Johns Hopkins University Press, 1996.

Marvin, C.
    When Old Technologies Were New: Thinking about Communication in the Late Nineteenth Century. New York: Oxford University Press, 1988.

Massey, D.
    Space, Place and Gender. Cambridge, Mass.: Polity Press, 1994.

McLaughlin, L.
    Feminist Communication Scholarship and "The Woman Question" in the Academy. *Communication Theory* 5 (1995): 144–61.

Miller, T.
    The Well-Tempered Self: Citizenship, Culture and the Postmodern Subject. Baltimore: Johns Hopkins University Press, 1993.

Mitra, A.
    Virtual Commonality: Looking for India on the Internet. In S. Jones (Ed.), *Virtual Culture: Identity and Communication in Cybersociety,* 55–79. London: Sage, 1997.

Mohanty, C. T.
    Under Western Eyes: Feminist Scholarship and Colonial Discourses. In P. Williams & L. Chrisman (Eds.), *Colonial Discourse and Post-Colonial Theory: A Reader,* 196–220. New York: Columbia University Press, 1994.

Mohanty, C. T.
    Defining Genealogies: Feminist Reflections on Being South Asian in North America. In the Women of South Asian Descent Collective (Eds.), *Our Feet Walk the Sky: Women of the South Asian Diaspora,* 351–58. San Francisco, Calif.: Aunt Lute Books, 1993.

Munt, S. R. (Ed.).
    Technospaces: Inside the New Media. New York: Continuum, 2001.

Nakamura, L.
    Cybertypes: Race, Ethnicity, and Identity on the Internet. New York: Routledge, 2002.

REFERENCES

Nakayama, T. K.
Disciplining Evidence. *Western Journal of Communication* 59 (1995): 171–75.

Narayan, K.
How Native Is a "Native" Anthropologist? In L. Lamphere, H. Ragone, & P. Zavella (Eds.), *Situated Lives: Gender and Culture in Everyday Life,* 23–41. New York: Routledge, 1997.

Narayan, U.
The Project of Feminist Epistemology: Perspectives from a Nonwestern Feminist. In A. M. Jaggar & S. R. Bordo (Eds.), *Gender/Body/Knowledge: Feminist Reconstructions of Being a Knowing,* 256–72. Piscataway, N.J.: Rutgers University Press, 1990.

Nayak, A.
The Hybrid Cultures of Cyborg Diasporas: Making Sense of the Conversations of the Expatriate Odia Community on the Internet. Unpublished manuscript, 2002.

Nelson, J. S., Megill, A., & McCloskey, D. N. (Eds.).
The Rhetoric of the Human Sciences: Language and Argument in Scholarship and Public Affairs. Madison: University of Wisconsin Press, 1987.

Ong, A.
Flexible Citizenship. Durham, N.C.: Duke University Press, 1999.

Press, A., & Cole, E.
Speaking of Abortion: Television and Authority in the Lives of Women. Chicago: University of Chicago Press, 1999.

Rai, A. S.
India On-line: Electronic Bulletin Boards and the Construction of a Diasporic Hindu Identity. *Diaspora* 4, no. 1 (1995): 31–57.

Rakow, L. F.
Gendered Technology, Gendered Practice. *Critical Studies in Mass Communication* 5 (1988): 57–70.

Reed, L.
Domesticating the Personal Computer: The Mainstreaming of a New Technology and the Cultural Management of a Widespread Technophobia. *Critical Studies in Media Communication* 17, no. 2 (2000): 159–85.

Rheingold, H.
Virtual Reality. New York: Touchstone, 1991.

Sadowski-Smith, C.
U.S. Border Theory, Globalization, and Ethnonationalisms in Post-Wall Eastern Europe. *Diaspora* 8, no. 1 (1999): 3–22.

Said, E. W.
Orientalism. New York: Pantheon Books, 1978.

Sangari, K. K., & Vaid, S.
Recasting Women. New Delhi: Kali for Women, 1989.

Sassen, S.
Globalization and Its Discontents. New York: New Press, 1998.

Sauer, C.
Removing the Mask of Silence: Counteracting Gender Bias through a Cybergirl Classroom. Doctoral diss., Bowling Green State University, 2001.

Schiller, D.
From Culture to Information and Back Again: Commoditization As a Route to Knowledge. *Critical Studies in Mass Communication* 11 (1994): 92–115.

Schiller, H. I.
Not Yet the Post-Imperialist Era. *Critical Studies in Mass Communication* 8 (1991): 13–28.

Schiller, N., Basch, L., & Blanc-Szanton, C. (Eds.).
Towards a Transnational Perspective on Migration: Race, Class, Ethnicity, and Nationalism Reconsidered. New York: The New York Academy of Science, 1992.

Senft, T. M.
Introduction: Performing the Digital Body—A Ghost Story [Electronic version]. *Women and Performance: A Journal of Feminist Theory* 1, no. 17 (2003). Retrieved November 3, 2003, from http://www.echonyc.com/~women/Issue17/introduction.html.

Sharma, A.
Girl Seeks "Suitable Boy": An Introduction. Paper presented at the Association of Internet Researchers Annual Conference, Toronto, Ontario, 2003.

Shiva, V.
Close to Home: Women Reconnect Ecology, Health and Development. India: Kali for Women, 1994.

Sholle, D. J.
Critical Studies: From the Theory of Ideology to Power/Knowledge. *Critical Studies in Mass Communication* 5 (1988): 16–41.

REFERENCES

Shome, R.
Caught in the Term "Post-Colonial": Why the "Post-Colonial" Still Matters. *Critical Studies in Mass Communication* 15, no. 2 (1998): 203–12.

Shome, R.
Postcolonial Interventions in the Rhetorical Canon: An "Other" View. *Communication Theory* 6, no. 1 (1996): 40–59.

Slack, J. D.
Contextualizing Technology. In B. Dervin, L. Grossberg, B. O'Keefe, & E. Wartella (Eds.), *Rethinking Communication Volume 2, Paradigm/Exemplars*, 329–45. Newbury Park, Calif.: Sage, 1989.

Slack, J. D.
Programming Protection: The Problem of Software. *Journal of Communication* 31 (1981): 151–63.

Slack, J. D., & Allor, M.
The Political and Epistemological Constituents of Critical Communication Research. *Journal of Communication* 33 (1983): 208–18.

Spender, D.
Nattering on the Net: Women, Power and Cyberspace. North Melbourne, Australia: Spinifex, 1995.

Spivak, G. C.
A Critique of Postcolonial Reason: Toward a History of the Vanishing Present. Cambridge, Mass.: Harvard University Press, 1999.

Spivak, G. C.
"Woman" as Theater: United Nations Conference on Women, Beijing 1995. *Radical Philosophy* 75 (January–February 1996): 2–4.

Spivak, G. C.
Can the Subaltern Speak? In P. Williams & L. Chrisman (Eds.), *Colonial Discourse and Post-Colonial Theory: A Reader*, 66–111. New York: Columbia University Press, 1994.

Spivak, G. C., & Grosz, E.
Criticism, Feminism, and the Institution. In S. Harasym (Ed.), *The Postcolonial Critic: Interviews, Strategies, Dialogues*, 1–16. New York: Routledge, 1990.

Stabile, C. A.
Resistance, Recuperation, and Reflexivity: The Limits of a Paradigm. *Critical Studies in Mass Communication* 12 (1995): 403–22.

Stabile, C. A.
Feminism and the Technological Fix. New York: Manchester University Press, 1994.

Stacey, J.
Can There Be a Feminist Ethnography? *Women's Studies International Forum* 11, no. 1 (1988): 21–27.

Stone, J. L.
Contextualizing Biogenetic and Reproductive Technologies. *Critical Studies in Mass Communication* 8 (1991): 309–32.

Strine, M. S.
Understanding "How Things Work": Sexual Harassment and Academic Culture. *Journal of Applied Communication Research* 20 (1992): 391–400.

Sudha, S.
Compu-Devata: Electronic Bulletin Boards and Political Debates. *SAMAR: South Asian Magazine for Action and Reflection* 2 (1993): 4–10.

Sunden, J.
What Happened to Difference in Cyberspace? The (Re)turn of the She-Cyborg. *Feminist Media Studies* 1, no. 2 (2001): 215–32.

Van Zoonen, L.
Feminist Internet Studies. *Feminist Media Studies* 1, no. 1 (2001): 67–72.

Visweswaran, Kamala.
Fictions of Feminist Ethnography. Minneapolis: University of Minnesota Press, 1994.

Vitanza, V.
Cyberreader. Boston: Allyn and Bacon, 1999.

Wander, P. C.
Introduction: Special Issue on Ideology. *Western Journal of Communication* 57 (1993): 105–10.

Wander, P.
The Politics of Despair. *Communication* 11 (1990): 277–90.

Wander, P.
The Third Persona: An Ideological Turn in Rhetorical Theory. *Central States Speech Journal* 35 (1984): 197–216.

REFERENCES

Wander, P.
    The Ideological Turn in Modern Criticism. *Central States Speech Journal* 34 (1983): 1–18.

Ward, K. J.
    The Cyber-Ethnographic (Re)construction of Two Feminist Online Communities. *Sociological Research Online* 4, no. 1 (1999). Retrieved November 3, 2003, from http://www.socresonline.org.uk/socresonline/4/1/ward.html.

Warnick, B.
    Masculinizing the Feminine: Inviting Women on line 1997. *Critical Studies in Mass Communication* 16 (1999): 1–19.

Wilding, F., & Fernandez, M.
    Feminism, Difference, and Global Capital. In C. Sollfrank and Old Boys Network (Eds.), *Next Cyberfeminist International*, 22–24. Hamburg: Hem & Co., 1999.

INDEX

ABOUT THE AUTHOR

Radhika Gajjala (Ph.D., University of Pittsburgh, 1998) is associate professor in interpersonal communication/communication studies at Bowling Green State University, Ohio. Her research interests include information communication technologies (ICTs) and globalization. She teaches courses on cyber culture, humanistic research methods, and feminist research methods in communication. Her research interests include new media technologies, critical theory, feminist theory, transnational communication, and postcolonial theory. She is a member of the Spoon Collective and runs several online lists related to gender and postcolonial theory. Since 1997 she has also been collaborating—both through Internet dialogue and through engagement in the field—with NGO fieldworkers examining alternative developmental models in order to benefit handloom weavers in South India. Her work has appeared in journals such as *Feminist Media Studies, International and Intercultural Annual, Contemporary South Asia,* and *Works and Days,* and in books such as *Technospaces: Inside the New Media* (2001) and *Domain Errors! Cyberfeminist Practices* (2003). Professional URL: http://personal.bgsu.edu/~radhik.

ABOUT THE AUTHOR

Annapurna Mamidipudi, an engineering graduate, is a founding trustee of Dastkar Andhra, an NGO working with strengthening the handloom industry in Andhra Pradesh, established in 1988. She has coordinated the technical training program in natural dyes for craft groups in India and abroad since 1990. Her work with Dastkar Andhra has included setting up production delivery and market linkages for producer groups and co-operatives, and setting up of DAMA, the marketing wing of Dastkar Andhra, which provides design, product development, and marketing services to handloom weavers.